Contents

EDUCATION 2000

A CONSULTATIVE DOCUMENT ON
HYPOTHESES FOR EDUCATION
IN AD 2000

being an anthology of papers written at
a residential conference
at Westfield College 1–8 July 1983

CAMBRIDGE UNIVERSITY PRESS

Cambridge
London   New York   New Rochelle
Melbourne   Sydney

Published by the Press Syndicate of the University of Cambridge
The Pitt Building, Trumpington Street, Cambridge CB2 1RP
32 East 57th Street, New York, NY 10022, USA
296 Beaconsfield Parade, Middle Park, Melbourne 3206, Australia

First published 1983

Printed in Great Britain by the University Press, Cambridge

Library of Congress catalogue card number: 83—17132

British Library Cataloguing in Publication Data
Education 2000.
1. Education—Great Britain—1965—Congresses
I. Thwaites, Bryan
370'.941 LA632

ISBN 0 521 27821 X

This consultative document

has been compiled under the auspices of

The trustees of Education 2000

The document consists of nine independent papers arranged in a more-or-less logical order. The authors of each paper are named at its head. On most matters there emerged a remarkable degree of unaniminity within the whole conference. But naturally, no one individual will subscribe to every point of view expressed in this document; and no one member has been contributive as a delegate from any other organisation.

The trustees express their profound gratitude to the conference members for having set aside a whole week from their normal responsibilities to produce, with so much hard labour and with such an extraordinary degree of consensus, this consultative document; and particularly to those who chaired the groups so expertly, respectively:

1 Mr Albert E. Dodd   5 Mr Michael N. Duffy
2 Mr David Peacock   6 Mr John R. K. Sayer
3 Miss Diana Whittingham   7 Mr Eric A. G. Morgan
4 Dr John G. Axford   8 Mr Tim R. P. Brighouse
9 Dr Ray M. W. Rickett

Education 2000 is a Registered Charitable Educational Trust

Its work is founded upon three assumptions
which will animate its activities over the coming years.

These assumptions are:

1   The structures and methods of education must help to sustain the traditional values of society; but they must also respond adequately to the current and future rates of cultural, social, industrial and technological change.
2   These rates of change will be such that every individual of whatever capability will need access to educational opportunities throughout life; and these opportunities should not be limited, as has been the convention, mainly to childhood and adolescence.
3   Given that the typical lead-time for the implementation of major educational reform is at present of the order of twenty years, it is a matter of the greatest national importance that goals should now be set for education after AD 2000.

The trustees wish to express their warmest thanks to those individuals and firms whose generosity has enabled the completion of the 1983 conference.

Especially, the Trustees and all the conference members wish to offer their loyal appreciation of the patronage of the conference by His Royal Highness the Duke of Edinburgh whose suggestions did so much to shape the Conference's work.

EDUCATION 2000

The motivations for the 1983 conference

Everyone is concerned with education. Most have spent at least eleven years being educated and have then observed the effects of education on their children.

The working of the education service affects the lives of us all. The service has, of course, developed over the years; but during the next two decades the rate of change within it must sharply accelerate if it is to be in tune with the likely social and technological evolution of the United Kingdom.

The trustees of Education 2000 are aware that communication has not always been fruitful between those in the educational system and those outside it. They believe that it is now more than ever important that inter-communication should occur and be effective. To help it to be so, the trustees invited some 60 individuals with, between them, a wide variety of experience to form the 1983 working conference, held at Westfield College, University of London.

The nine papers of this consultative document were each produced by the people named at their heads. They are not intended to provide, between them, a single view. They are commended as being produced with the best of intentions and with the objective of giving those who wished an opportunity to join in discussion preparatory to a conference in 1984 on ways and means.

To begin with, three preliminary points need emphasis. First, the word 'education' is being used generally and in the broadest sense: the development of character and capabilities, the acquisition of specific skills, the enhancement of intellect (or mind, body and soul), and the training of the social human being. Only when there is a specialist meaning of the word is it explained. Second, we are not taking up any party political stance—indeed we have probably taken ideas from most shades of political opinion; and the main practical reason for this is that, during the time-scale of the implementation of the changes we wish to see come about, there could well be four or five governments of different political character. Third, we do not believe that change, even generally-agreed change, can take place overnight: the time-scales which are built in to the whole system are so long that (as experience has shown) a ten- to twenty-year time span is realistic. Hence our title Education 2000, referring to the end of this century. We believe, however, that the process of change must start now: after all, there are already children, a few years old, who will still be being educated in one way or another in fifteen to twenty years' time, and their parents can reasonably expect that proper plans are being made now for their future education.

Our first assumption, then, is: 'the structures and methods of education must help to sustain the traditional values of society; but they must also respond adequately to the current and future rates of cultural, social, industrial and technological change'. Two comments may be made on this. We do not define British society's traditional values, partly because in any event they gradually evolve as time goes by, and partly because ideological differences, and the contrasts within a pluralist society, seem somewhat sharper now than in recent decades. Nevertheless, we believe that most adults in our society possess a common instinct for what is good and best in communal behaviour, and that they wish their feelings to be carried forward to the next generation; and we believe that the home and family is, or perhaps should be, at least as influential as the school. And then we assert that the educational system must be structured to enable it to keep abreast of change in society in the large.

Our second assumption is: 'these rates of change will be such that every individual of whatever capability will need access to educational opportunities throughout life; and these opportunities should not be limited, as has been the convention, mainly to childhood and adolescence'. The combined thrust of the arguments laid out in the following chapters convince us that the concept of education as an experience to be almost totally concentrated on one's youth stems from the practicalities of the late nineteenth century and of the first Education Act of 1870, and has little to do with the patterns of life to be expected at the beginning of the twenty-first century.

Our third assumption is: 'given that the typical lead-time for the implementation of major educational reform is at present of the order of twenty years, it is a matter of the greatest national importance that goals should now be set for education after AD 2000'. Yet we are not aware of any concerted thought being given by the principal authorities involved to global strategies for education of a kind which might be embodied in a major Education Act.

The short history of state education makes this all the more surprising.

There were little more than seventy years between the first Act and the last of any importance (the Butler Act), and now that another forty years have gone by,there is little fresh in sight. Instead, there are myriads of totally unconnected reports and papers being produced all the time by large numbers of concerned organisations and associations, the effective result of which is very limited.

Why, you may therefore ask, have the trustees and many other busy people from all walks of life gone to the trouble of producing yet another document which, according to the precedents, will not be heeded? There are five answers to this.

First, this consultative document is the result of discussions involving an unusual breadth of interests. It emanates neither from the broad area of schools, nor from the universities or polytechnics, nor from commerce and industry: instead, people from many areas of national life have come together to share their ideas about education in the future.

Second, this consultative document, written as a result of a week's intensive residential work, is the only document (as far as we know) which attempts to examine the whole of the country's educational requirements in the context of a realisable time-scale and against the background of our society. Thus we have not limited our enquiry by subject or discipline, or by type of institution, or by age-groups, or by ability.

Third, the consequence of this comprehensive approach—namely the absence of the kind of detail over which individuals and committees argue endlessly—is that readers will be encouraged to lift their sights from the foreground, and to examine the distant outlines.

Fourth, we decided early on to eschew the 'Royal Commission' format of measured prose, of point and counterpoint, of statistical surveys and tables; and to produce instead a document which is relatively short, whose chief points (in the form of hypotheses) are instantly visualised on the page, and which is easily capable of wide circulation.

Fifth, this document is not intended to be definitive or prescriptive: the problems are too difficult for instant diagnosis and remedy. It is essentially a 'Green Paper' aimed at the nation at large. Education 2000 looks forward to receiving a major response to its invitation to comment on the following collection of papers; and it will plan its 1984 conference—aimed at determining a programme of action and influence up to about 1990—largely on the results of the consultations which will have been vigorously pursued in the period September 1983 to March 1984.

That, then, is the background of the present publication and the hopes for the future which rest upon it, and you are warmly invited to contribute your thoughts and reactions by writing to one of the co-chairmen mentioned on page xv.

Preface to the 1983 consultative document

Readers of this discussion document may be surprised, on their first reading, at certain apparent omissions in the conference's outcome. These arose for good reasons and it may be helpful to mention the most obvious.

First, then, while much of the discussion is in the context of England and Wales, many of the challenges being addressed relate to the whole of the United Kingdom. Perhaps more significant, however, is that not much attention is given to the impact of our country's close association with Western Europe and the United States. The reason for this is simple: education is complicated enough when considered only on the national scale: we judged that any profound examination of international comparisons and influences would have placed this year's work beyond the limits of practicality, but that next year the European connection (in particular) would have to be considered in some detail.

Second, there is not a great deal said about universities and polytechnics as such. This is partly due to a desire to try to emphasise the global aspect of an education system of which those two are a relatively small part; and partly because we envisage our work over the coming twelve months paying more attention to such minority parts of the whole system.

Third, little mention is made of money, or of financial resources. This is deliberate. At this stage, our concern is to hypothesise as to what may be feasible or desirable in fifteen to twenty years' time. When, 1n 1984, we make firmer conclusions and recommendations, the financial implications will be made clearer; and if they involve additional expenditure (which, at the moment, is not seen as inevitably the case), then the arguments will be backed by adequate financial predictions.

Fourth, the reader is invited to recognise that the normal usage of common phrases is not invariably carried over into the following text. A simple example lies in the use of the phrase 'furthur education' which is certainly not to be confused with FE as we know it at the moment.

No doubt there are other peculiarities which will strike one reader more forcibly than another. One thing, however, is clear: that the process of consultation during 1983/84 will elucidate the areas of omission as well as those of contention, and it will be one task of the 1984 conference to resolve the problems thus posed.

But there are also some very positive things to say about the 1983 conference. The first has already been touched upon: the membership not only spanned an unprecedented range of interests within our national life, but also found itself in a greater state of mutual harmony of ideas for the development of education in AD 2000 than had earlier been thought possible.

Next, the members found the format of hypotheses, discussions, special points, general comments and recommendations for each paper a positive aid to their discussions; and it is hoped that the reader will find it equally helpful in understanding the thrust of the thinking.

The volume of work, done from early morning to late at night and sustained for a full seven days, was, of course, stupendous. Nevertheless, such headlong writing is bound to result in inconsistencies, duplications, contradictions and infelicities. But these obvious deficiencies are to be set against what we believe is the far greater power of the agreements on major issues as reflected in the conference resolutions.

It is our hope that the sense of urgency and commitment which inspired the conference will inspire others to press ahead with the reforms which are so patently necessary.

Acknowledgements

The Members of the 1983 conference wish to record their profound gratitude to:

Miss Sue M. Lewis for her superbly efficient secretaryship, over many months, of Education 2000 and of the conference itself;

Colonel Patrick Pengelly for his splendid staff work during the meeting; the Westfield undergraduates—Miss Judith Gash, Mr P. J. Costello, Mr J. R. Honniball, Mr A. G. Jenkins and Mr Mark S. Smith—who operated the College's main-frame computer (in a word-processing mode) with much skill and willing hard work;

Westfield College, and its domestic staff, for the excellence of the food and of all the other facilities which were so unstintedly provided for the conference.

Follow-up

It has already been mentioned that the next twelve months will be devoted to sounding opinion, on a national scale, on the issues raised in this consultative document. In particular, the reader is invited to send comments to one or other of the two co-chairmen of Education 2000, namely:

Professor Bryan Thwaites,
The Department of Education,
The University of Southampton. SO9 5NH
Tel: (0703)-559122

Mr. Christopher R. W. Wysock Wright,
Wrightson Wood,
11, Grosvener Place,
London. SW1X 7HH
Tel: (01)-245-9871

A summary of issues and recommendations from the chairmen of the nine groups

1   A coordinated effort by the major educational, training and industrial bodies is urgently required to bring about the changes in the patterns and provisions of Education which our developing society needs over the coming two or three decades.

2   A major objective of such an effort would be to unlock the full talents of our fellow citizens which, we believe, are undervalued by the existing structures of Education and Employment.

3   The key issue is the replacement of the GCE and CSE examination systems by new methods of assessing from time to time the progress, capability and achievement of all young people.

4   The early years of education (for example, up to the age of 14) should be based on a partnership of home and school with a radically-revised curriculum designed to meet the needs of those, of all aptitudes, who will grow up in the coming decades of great technological development yet in a national society which adheres to traditional values.

5   Between such an age and the legal age of majority, young people should be entitled, without financial detriment, to a mixed programme of individual education, training, and work experience, according to their needs and requirements, and to local and national circumstances.

6   Legislation should entitle (within reasonable financial constraints) adults of any age to further education, training or re-training.

7   Education 2000 should, during the coming months, seek national support for the above objectives; and that, whether by conference or otherwise, it should draw up a second consultative document in 1984 aimed at proposing the methods by which these and other objectives might be acheived by AD 2000.

SOCIETY IN AD 2000

This paper was written by:
Mr David Kershaw,
  Head of Coundon Court Comprehensive School, Coventry
Chief Superintendent B. H. Skitt BEM,
  Head of Planning Branch-Metropolitan Police Training
Dr Jim Stevenson,
  Education Secretary, BBC
Dr J. Verner Wheelock,
  *Chairman Postgraduate School of Science and Society,
  University of Bradford*

under the chairmanship of:
Mr Albert E. Dodd,
  Company Personnel and Industrial Relations Manager, Ferranti

Hypotheses and their discussions

H1.1: Provided wise decisions are taken and a constructive approach is adopted, the United Kingdom will continue to be a relatively highly developed and wealthy nation.

D1.1: Society and the economy are continually changing. We use resources and discover and develop new ones. Attitudes change, new technologies are introduced, markets evolve and the pattern of employment is in a continual state of flux.

About 400 years ago, most of the workforce was engaged in food production—today there is less than 3 per cent engaged in farming.

It was during the Industrial Revolution that society experienced profound changes in coping with the very different requirements demanded by an economy in which the manufacturing industry became the

1

predominant form of employment rather than farming. Changes included: the growth and establishment of urban areas, the growth of the formal economy (i.e. use of money) and the acceptance of the discipline essential to the success of the manufacturing industry.

It has even been suggested that the primary purpose of education for the industrial society was to instil the characteristics obedience, repetition and punctuality. Without these the manufacturing industry could not function effectively!

Today, all the indications are that because of the enormous potential for increased productivity made available by new technologies we are moving out of the industrial era (i.e. one in which a major form of employment is the manufacturing industry) and into a 'post-industrial' era. This does not mean the end of the manufacturing industry but the beginning of an era in which the number of employees required to produce the material goods is significantly reduced. We are about to witness similar changes in routine clerical work.

Consequently we are in a state of transition in which we are experiencing another major change in the framework of society. Unlike the development of the industrial era, which had its traumas, the rate of change is very rapid. This means the time for adaptation is short.

To cope effectively it is important to make wise decisions. However, the difficulties of doing so are exacerbated because the societal framework is changing. It is an essential aspect of contemporary decision-making that we recognise this changing framework and attempt to understand how the parameters are shifting.

We all have basic needs for food, shelter and clothing, but in modern society the quality of life is enhanced by having access to a wide range of consumer goods and services. In essence the wealth of the nation is dependent on the degree of such access and the success of viable home-based companies in competition for markets both at home and abroad.

If this country is to remain an active participant in the international trading community it is essential that British companies earn foreign exchange to pay for the imports we wish to purchase. The alternative would be a siege economy with tight foreign exchange control and no imports or foreign travel. By 2000 the British economy will have to cope with the effect of declining supplies of North Sea oil. In addition the international economy is likely to experience severe strains if the gap between the rich and the poor countries continues to grow.

It is important to realise that foreign exchange can be earned in a variety of different ways which include: export of food, manufactured goods, energy, selling services, and even knowledge through software, books, tapes, TV programmes, distance learning materials, overseas students training in Britain and the provision of consulting services.

Success (or survival) in business is dependent on making a profit for future development. This in turn means identifying a demand and meeting it as fully as possible. As the economy is continually evolving, some markets go into decline but new opportunities arise constantly. Therefore it is essential to try to understand how the pattern of markets is changing, and often necessary to predict markets years in advance because of the lead-time in getting a new product on to the market.

In deciding which markets to enter, companies have to assess the availability of resources. Britain has enormous existing and potential human resources, but these have to be developed. This means that education and training are critical. Furthermore, great care must be taken to match individuals to the requirements of specific jobs.

In contemporary society, the economy is influenced by government in a variety of ways. These include legislation, taxation and spending patterns.

Many government decisions are taken with a single objective in view, but when put into effect they conflict with a completely different objective being encouraged by another arm of government. Others are based on a false interpretation of the framework. Many fail to take account of uncertainty and there are numerous examples of consecutive conflicting decisions.

Decisions of this kind are counter-productive, may lead to inefficient use of resources, and have an adverse effect on the ability of the country to create wealth.

We argue that one of the reasons for the poor quality of decision making is that many executives suffer from 'tunnel vision'; a direct result of the emphasis on specialisation in contemporary education. This condition is reinforced by the difficulty of moving between sectors, e.g. from industry to the civil service or from commerce to education.

In education too we have a closed introspective loop. Very few teachers have experience outside the system in other forms of employment and this inevitably means that most teachers have a relatively limited view of society as a whole, let alone the changes which are currently taking place. If the teaching profession itself is rigid, we cannot expect the teachers to stimulate and develop the skills, aptitudes and confidence necessary to cope effectively with change.

Every effort must be made by private firms, institutions, government and the individuals themselves to facilitate movement from one job to another and one skill to another.

If we appreciate the reasons for change and understand how to respond, then most people can expect a stimulating and fulfilling future provided there is a degree of goal harmonisation between groups. Failure to cope with the considerable changes will mean that the country becomes poorer in relative terms and probably in real terms.

H1.2: Change will be the normal state of a society and society must prepare itself as well as it can for such change.

D1.2: The rate of significant change affecting society will increase dramatically in the remainder of the century, to such an extent that change itself will come to be accepted as a normal part of life. The ramifications of change will dramatically affect all our institutions, particularly education and all sides of industry and commerce and the public services.

The nature of work will change profoundly. Employment in traditional industries will decline at an ever increasing rate as the impact of the new technologies spreads across the blue-collar and into the white-collar areas throughout the economy. Traditional factory employment for large numbers working on simple repetitive processes will be recognised to have been a transient source of human employment. The clerk will lose many tasks to the microcomputer. New sources of employment will spring up which are still impossible to identify but based on technologies already developing—microprocessors, communications technology, bio-engineering, non-fossil fuel energy, robotics and the service and supply industries that will develop around them. It is unlikely that we will successfully compete internationally in these areas without a degree of planning that matches that of our overseas competitors and without a concerted effort to encourage able youngsters to develop skills and careers in these areas. Properly exploited, the new technologies will generate wealth for future generations in the UK but not necessarily jobs on a large scale, unlike manufacturing industry in the nineteenth and twentieth centuries. If we are to encourage the populace to move from the old to the new forms of employment there will have to be a rapid build up of small business opportunities across the whole spectrum of human activity. The ideas will be generated if we encourage the entrepreneurs and they are backed up by teams motivated by the small business ethic of self reliance.

Responding to such changes, education will adapt, but continue to provide essential basic preparation and opportunities for retraining throughout life. The changes in the educational system will be profound. For the first time the nation is facing the prospect of young people, disenchanted with their school experience, with the prospect of no job to go to. Schools

4

and the whole community of post-secondary education and training will have to rise to this challenge.

It will be necessary to acknowledge that in providing educational opportunities for young and old it is right to prepare people for a life in which work still plays a significant part and which involves commitment. In return employers will acknowledge that, in the year 2000, employees will be led but not driven to respond enthusiastically when given the chance to contribute constructively.

Education will continue to be supported by the state, but the involvement of private agencies and independent groups, including the community at large, will have expanded out of all recognition. Throughout the changes there will be a searching and detailed questioning of the effectiveness and quality of education.

Education will play a major part in smoothing the passage into the post-industrial era, but we cannot expect education alone to solve the problems of society.

The nature of the family will continue to evolve with smaller families started later in life, more one-parent families and families separated geographically over large areas. This continued disintegration of the nuclear family will place additional strains on the social services.

All sections of society will be faced with the prospect of increased leisure time, a tendency apparent for centuries but much more in evidence by the year 2000. The development of leisure industries will make a significant contribution to the numbers employed, and training for leisure will make demands on the educational system. However, unlimited leisure time will prove to be an ineffective and unfulfilling alternative to gainful employment.

H1.3: This country has a notable history of tolerance, moderation and care which gives us confidence that the normal feedback mechanisms operative in society will prevent swings to any extreme of political activity or the demise of the concept of care.

D1.3: We are, by reason of the experience of centuries, less likely to accept any major swing to the extremes of political activity, whether in the form of policy or practical demonstrations of open opposition involving large-scale public disorder.

It appears evident that there is public disenchantment with policies involving confrontation and extremism. There is a developing move towards cooperation and consensus. However, it would be foolish to be

5

complacent. Historically the evidence would seem to show that whilst we have always reacted fiercely to the threat of external aggression, we have been able to absorb internal differences without generating strife. The likelihood of demonstrations of opposition is not in itself alarming unless the scale is of such a degree as to be indicative of an inherent instability, which we consider unlikely. For example, the often perceived stance of trade unions and employees is moving away from the argument for obtaining a greater share of the wealth towards the need to produce it. Equally employers have begun to recognise that their workers are a positive asset to their enterprise and are entitled to share in its success. Even the significant increase in unemployment has failed in part to make an impact and we have seen the repeated rejection of the views of those who have sought confrontation as a response.

There will be those who, for geographical, cultural, or financial reasons, will continue to feel seriously disadvantaged and some positive support for them will be essential.

There must be a continuing commitment to the care of those who for reasons of health or circumstance are less able to fend for themselves. It is suggested that we are a basically caring society but this assumption must be viewed against the hypothesis that people will increasingly exercise their own individual interests to the possible detriment of others. Nevertheless it has also to be emphasised that increasing realism and acceptance of the basic laws governing our financial affairs must dictate that the amount of care will be expressed in terms of the wealth available to support it, within a framework of efficiency and accountability. There will need to be a similar acknowledgement in educational establishments.

As a society we shall place great emphasis on efficiency, but concomitant with efficiency is inherent vulnerability. Efficiency in systems and organisations puts great power into the hands of small groups of people. This risk must be recognised.

H1.4: People will increasingly exercise their own individual interests and priorities in adapting to their social situation; work, study and leisure activities.

D1.4: Education has not, for many years, been the exclusive preserve of schools, colleges and universities. Outside such institutions, people in Britain and Western Europe live in an environment which is educationally rich and the gradual extension of the range of learning materials available has led to greater educational diversity and opportunity. Education of all sorts can be bought off the shelf, absorbed through the media, extended to everyone, and need no longer be cocooned in conventional classes at defined ages.

In the past decade much attention has been given to the individual learners studying at their own pace. For adults the Open University has encouraged teaching at a distance with students in control of their own learning resources. And in schools the characteristic classroom atmosphere has begun to deformalise to the extent that pupils of differing abilities can develop at their own pace side by side without threat or boredom. There is a tendency towards more individual control and choice.

The new technologies encourage this, beginning with simple programmed learning in the sixties, through multi-media packages of learning materials in the seventies; the eighties are characterised, in education, by interactive software, video and the ubiquitous sound cassette. These, coupled with the increasingly attractive printed word, give both teacher and learner a range of effective resources upon which to draw.

The extension of these trends means that more people will be able to learn more over whatever time-scale they wish. Schooling might be continued throughout life. Training and retraining might be telescoped within specific points in a life. The characteristic will be flexibility. And with flexibility the need for formal congregation in groups will be less apparent. Just as the collective chanting of mathematical tables by rows of uniformed children has vanished so also will the manned vehicle assembly line, possibly the mass meeting and even someday the football crowd. Perhaps generations are growing up who do not necessarily assume that acting in unison is the norm.

For the passive consumer the new technologies have brought change also. The rate of penetration of each new invention surprises even the most optimistic salesmen. A thousand new microcomputers are bought by secondary schools every week. The video cassette recorder is now quite normal in British homes; in some communities it has reached almost 100 per cent. With cable and satellite communication just around the corner the potential information flow into every home becomes formidable. So not only education but also entertainment becomes more and more under the control of the user.

The end result of more readily available entertainment and learning resources must mean that people's awareness of social change and their ability to cope with it increases. There is a growing acceptance that in a working life two or more separate careers will be normal. The assumption of flexibility and the awareness of change will assist this. If the middle-aged are as actively learning as the teenagers then the old concepts of the phases of life might be eroded. The boundaries between childhood and adolescence

7

(the learning time), career (the time for work), and retirement (for rest) will dissolve. And as society begins to accept that the wealth of the nation can be maintained by a smaller amount of human activity, then a person's wealth-generating work will become less distinct from his or her wealth-consuming activity.

LIFELONG EDUCATION

This paper was written by:
Mrs Elsa Davies,
  Director, British Educational Management & Administration Society, Uxbridge
Mr Derek J. Fulford,
  English/Drama Advisor, Humberside County Council
Mr Peter Linklater,
  Chairman, The Careers Research Advisory Centre
Mr Nicholas J. Small
  Staff Tutor-Education Studies, Open University, Yorkshire Region

under the chairmanship of:
Mr David Peacock,
  Director, Institute of European Education, St Martin's College, Lancaster

Hypotheses and their discussions

H2.1: Society's aim will be to make the educational process acceptable to all and available, as of right, on a lifelong basis.

D2.1: People are the greatest resource available to any society. The development of their creativity, ingenuity and adaptability enlarges the choices and opportunities for members of that society to promote their talents and to fulfil their potential. At present, many educational opportunities exist differentially across British society.

Society will have to come to terms with the implications of change by providing suitable facilities, and by taking positive steps to encourage their use. Recognising the *unprecedented* and *rapid* changes that will affect society over the next two decades, a planned and coordinated pattern of educational provision across all age-groups is required.

9

Experience of education, work and leisure will not relate to life stages of growth, maturity and ageing; there will be much more interleaving to accommodate retraining, updating or new interests, both personal and professional. With greater life expectancy but a shorter working life, a shorter working week and changing employment opportunities, occupation and the work ethic will decline in importance for many individuals to be replaced by greater time spent on family and personal matters. Most people will be working as hard as ever, though many people will have more free time than now. Some will need constant encouragement not only to participate in society to the full but also to feel that they are making a worthwhile and acceptable contribution to society and their community, in the absence of the structure, framework and status conferred by paid employment.

The immediate priority is to make available to all throughout the country educational opportunities that are at present available only to some. This will require the switching of resource between and across educational sectors (though not necessarily greater total financial outlay) to set up an educational system available to all ages, all cultural groups and at all levels of educational achievement. Initially, the 'evening up' process, geographical and social, to achieve this may lead to a reduction of opportunities for some in order to extend minimal provision to all, especially to those in remote areas.

Central government policy across ministries and departments will need to be much more closely coordinated and systematised. For example, extended provision for young children requires a joint service covering health, education and social welfare.

The widespread application of available and future technology could allow much additional provision of educational opportunity at minimum cost to the system. Many people will rent or purchase advanced hardware which can be used for educational, leisure- or work-related purposes. So, in many instances, educational provision will consist of materials used at home, work or at a social centre. There is the prospect of courses, created by selecting from existing resources, tailored to individuals or small groups. Some forms of learning are best effected in groups for both adults and children.

The concept of the availability of education throughout life has to be implanted in the minds and experience of younger age-groups so that they are willing returners to learning. Essential pre-requisites are constant and easy access to information on educational opportunities and to a national network of educational guidance and counselling services. Thus, individual

10

aspirations and potential can be realised to the benefit of the community and society at large.

The perception of education's role and place in society will alter; and the significance of education in the lives of individuals will be enlarged. If society is not to fragment, nor industry decline, a necessarily expanded contribution of education in the life of all society's members must be acknowledged and relentlessly pursued.

H2.2: The education service will respond to the growing tendency for pupils' participation in education to depend upon their willingness and motivation rather than on custom or law.

D2.2: The tendency of pupils to make a choice whether to engage in education increases with age and now shows itself most clearly in the period immediately following compulsory schooling.

One of the reasons some children leave schools as soon as they are permitted is financial. Remuneration should be made to regularly engaged pupils who, if they had opted out of the education service, would qualify for social benefit.

For most pupils, however, the solution to the problem of disengagement has to be found within the formal provision. A proportion of older pupils can be persuaded, at least in the short term, that their education is useful. Achieving the immediate goal of passing and taking a number of examinations, preferably with good trading value, is perceived by them as worth working for: the certificates may act as a passport, if not a ticket, to favoured employment or a course of study.

The minority who find school work most difficult are commonly satisfied—where provision for them is sympathetic and adequate, as it often is—that they are being helped towards some skill in reading and social competence.

The middle group, of nearly 40 per cent, who at present succeed in no public examination, or no examination of significance when seeking employment, is now the most disgruntled. They will have to be offered an education throughout their school lives that they can appreciate as being interesting and helpful *at the time they receive it* if they are to partake regularly and return willingly in later years. If they are satisfied, then their more advanced contemporaries will become increasingly critical of what they are taught and may challenge its day-to-day appropriateness.

There will need to be a much greater willingness on the part of the education system to respond to the views of pupils, individually

11

and collectively, as well as to the views of parents, employers and others.

The changes that come from the response will require a great diversity of places where educational programmes are undertaken. In addition to schools, education may occur in homes, in colleges of further education, in workplaces and other institutions to a far greater extent than now.

H2.3: Up to the completion of the period of general education there will be major development of educational programmes encouraging the competence, confidence and self-determination of the learner within a social context.

D2.3: General education begins at birth and ends when the young person can make an informed choice between:

(a)   deferring further education until its use is perceived to be relevant to individual need; and

(b)   moving on to a more broadly based course of education and/or training which is more specifically geared to individual talents and aspirations.

For children and their parents, early learning takes place within the general social context of the family. To enhance this learning, better coordinated support involving social, medical, educational services, etc. needs to be provided for young families. Provision, for example in the form of local centres, and re-organised resources should be made available to give positive encouragement to such learning and to ease the transition from home to more organised learning.

During the period of general education, the social context of learning is important for the shared understanding it brings of the way in which the community and the wider society work and for its encouragement of mutual respect between people of diverse backgrounds. General education should also take account of the interests and capacities of individuals, the industrial and technological nature of the society within which they live and the resources available for teaching and learning. Experiential learning in areas of personal enrichment and creativity is essential, among other things so as to provide the impetus for the acquisition and application of skills including those of literacy and numeracy. Within this framework, a greater responsibility is placed on the teacher to devise learning programmes which both respond to the child's needs and encourage individual confidence, competence and self-determination.

Pupils, parents and teachers will be involved in the assessment of a pupil's progress. The assessment will be used throughout the period of

12

general education and will be necessary to promote efficient learning and essential for making an informed decision regarding the next stage of a person's life.

H2.4: Between the completion of the period of general education and whatever is the age of majority, young people will have the opportunity to avail themselves of further education and/or training on a part-time or full-time basis related to individual need.

D2.4: The period with which we are concerned here should be recognised as a bridging period between a general education and the start of higher education or work.

The age of the individual at the start of this bridging period will vary both with the ability and characteristics of the individual, and with his or her aspirations for the future. For similar reasons, the length of the bridging period may vary, from zero to several years after the completion of general education. The individual should be entitled to use one or other of the 'bridges' defined below. If he has no employer, he should receive from the state some form of monetary remuneration, provided that, if he had opted for unemployment, he would have been entitled to social security benefit.

The 'bridges' follow current or intended practice, and will include:

(a)   following a fairly academic process, in an establishment such as a school or sixth form college, with a degree of specialisation determined by the entrance qualifications to the higher education course intended to be pursued at a university, polytechnic, or elsewhere; this course will in some cases be part of a sponsorship or professional apprenticeship;

(b)   employment, with part-time education, of which part is general and part is vocational;

(c)   a full-time apprenticeship, involving manual and/or mental skills, the latter at either in the broadest sense of the word technician level, or professional level;

(d)   full- or part-time education or vocational training, at an institution such as a school or college of further education, which may or may not lead to paper qualifications;

(e)   full- or part-time courses, broadly of the sort envisaged in the 1983 Youth Training Scheme, with part extending the general education process, part vocational, and part giving work experience.

Entrance qualifications will as now be required for entry to some of these

13

'bridges'. To continue beyond the age of majority, acceptable qualifications and/or levels of competence will be required.

H2.5: There will be a much wider entry into higher education with substantial increase in both direct entry from further education into degree courses and entry by mature students on a full-time and part-time basis.

D2.5: In Great Britain, the participation rate in higher education is about 11 per cent. A comparable figure for the countries with which we compete would be nearer 30 per cent.

In 1980, 25 per cent of the school leavers had five or more O-levels and a further 10 per cent had three or four. Only 16 per cent of these school leavers had also acquired one or more A-levels and this had been the determining factor whether they entered higher education.

It is now widely argued that O-level performance is a better predictor of degree-level success at university/polytechnic than A-levels—where social background and a level of teaching not available in many schools, exercise disproportionate effect.

It is therefore contended that about 30 per cent of the rising generation would benefit from higher education and, in most cases, bring benefit to the economy in return.

Longer courses in other countries and a much higher drop-out rate (sometimes with credits) do not detract from a situation where the proportion of the rising generation that has studied at university, polytechnic or college of higher education is *at least twice* as high as in Great Britain.

When it is realised that the British proportion of 40 per cent of undergraduate entry reading science and engineering applies to equivalent entry in other countries, it follows that other national economies have been able to draw on a much larger pool of scientifically trained manpower even though some of this has been at lower level of attainment and comparable to the much depleted technician grade in Great Britain.

This wider diffusion of experience of higher education elsewhere has arguably produced more flexible and adaptable populations; it could also explain why skill shortages and resistance to change have proved unique handicaps to the progress of the UK economy since World War 2.

The cost of such an expansion of undergraduate entry could be contained or mitigated by measures such as the adoption of the Leverhulme Research on Higher Education proposals for more general, mandatory grant, two year ordinary degree courses (discretionary grants, loans or

14

employer sponsorships for honours degrees thereafter) and the preparedness of universities to increase their proportion of students living at home. Many youngsters would benefit from a break between school and university and deferring entrance for a proportion of intake should be cost-effective in ensuring maximum benefit from short degree courses.

UK higher education at both undergraduate- and postgraduate-level has an exceptionally high ratio of staff to students and we already spend a proportion of GNP on education which is comparable to our competitors. The capacity for expansion already exists by re-ordering priorities within the higher education system itself, and by adopting distance learning techniques and other flexible approaches.

A further consideration is the fact that the number of UK mature students (particularly those taking part-time degrees) is less than half the equivalent in USA or Canada. It is only very recently that recognition of experience as an alternative to academic qualifications, credit transfer provisions and 'Bridges to Learning' courses have begun to tap a major new source of recruitment to higher education. When combined with the new emphasis on professional up-dating, such as the new PICKUP (Professional, Industrial, and Commercial Up-dating) initiative by the Department of Education and Science, it is clear that considerable expansion in this area could be achieved quite quickly.

H2.6: Periodic retraining to acquire new or extended skills and knowledge will be necessary in many occupations, and continuing professional development will become mandatory for an increasing number of people.

D2.6: The concept of periodic retraining has been advocated by many authorities since Lord Bowden justified it in 1964.

Two basic factors create the need: the ever-increasing rate of change of technology, and changes in the economics of the world, country, or industry.

Technological changes in manufacturing industry may affect the product, or the processes of design, manufacture, management and administration. The advent of the microprocessor alone has caused retraining of many in service industries as well as in manufacturing.

Economic factors, sometimes coupled to technological change, will force changes in occupation.

Some individuals will choose to retrain: in order to become self-employed or to refresh and enliven their working lives.

New skills may be minor, for example the secretary may acquire

15

word-processing skills, while her boss needs keyboard skills to use the same equipment. But in many other cases a complete change in occupation results. The craftsman becomes a programmer or technician, mechanical engineers become electronic system designers. Such minor or major changes already affect many sections of the population. By AD 2000, anyone who wishes to work will need retraining at some time.

Intervals between retraining depend on circumstances. Some minor changes will occur at intervals of a year or two. In areas of very fast-moving technology, such as semiconductors, intervals between major changes are equally short. In other cases only one or two changes will take place in a working lifetime.

Opportunities and facilities for substantial retraining will largely be provided by the state. Where the individual is employed, agreement on the need, between employee and employer, will result in the cost, or a major part of it, being borne by the employer, who may also provide facilities. A grant system must continue for those not in employment.

In most professions, periodic retraining will be essential if the individual is to continue to practice effectively. This is particularly true for the teaching profession.

Initial training and retraining programmes in a particular area will often benefit by being conceived by the same people or organisation. Furthermore, wherever it is appropriate, initial trainees and retrainees with experience should learn together, to their mutual advantage.

Retraining in some cases is, and in more cases will be, mandatory. Continuing professional development is already mandatory for doctors and chartered surveyors, and the practice will spread to other self-regulating professions.

In most of the English-speaking world, an engineer must be registered if he wishes to practice in certain fields, particularly those affecting public health and safety. Finniston advocates similar compulsory registration, and also continuing 'formation' for all engineers. Before the year 2000, these recommendations will probably be implemented, either by statute or by the engineering institutions.

H2.7: There will be much greater involvement in education by individuals in pursuit of personal enrichment throughout their lives.

D2.7: There is evidence that a significant proportion of the adult population feel regret that their early education did not give them the opportunity for serious study on some area of general interest. Indeed, a

16

majority would now like to take up some course quite unrelated to their work, if the right opportunity and circumstances occurred. A surprising number already do so, and, in so doing, surmount substantial barriers. Moreover, as the amount of time spent by the population in remunerated employment decreases, the demand for self-determined activities will grow.

Individuals will choose to obtain personal enrichment through structuring their own programmes ranging from passive interest to active exchanges. These will take place at a variety of locations and will involve local, regional, national, and supra-national agencies. They will be of varying duration and may be residential. Such programmes may embrace opportunities for recreation, including intellectual stimulation, which result in a sense of well-being and achievement. Areas might reasonably cover a range of activities from fell walking to paper hanging and from art appreciation to language learning.

Some groups may identify themselves by cultural or other common-interest patterns. Again, they could be consciously invigorated by the prospect of tackling something entirely outside their previous life experience.

It must be borne in mind that increasing provision in the ways envisaged here will itself have some important consequences that cause difficulty. Enabling people to develop new skills in music making leads to a demand for opportunities to perform. An increase in the number of people visiting places of interest, natural or man-made, may be more than these can bear without irreparable damage, or overcrowding to an extent that militates against enjoyment.

In addition to the sort of difficulties mentioned above, there is the overall problem of resourcing the provision needed to satisfy the growing demand.

Private provision for personal enrichment will continue to grow through the further development of commercially based enterprises and self-help groups such as the university of the Third Age. Some funds, moreover, may arise from the development of tourism, including those aspects generated within a civic or community context. By this is intended, for example, the specific investment of local finances to provide an attractive focus for local/national/international interest leading to a commercial return.

The complexity of this set of circumstances requires overall planning. Notwithstanding the additional provision offered by private arrangements, there will be a growing need for public support.

Sound economic sense suggests the adoption of a coordinated approach, locally and nationally, taking full account of provision, both public and private, as it may currently exist.

General conclusions

G2.1: The fundamental aim of the educational system should be to provide the climate and facilities to allow all individuals to realise the full potential of their capabilities and to encourage them to use these capabilities in every appropriate way both for the enrichment of their personal lives and for the benefit of society as a whole.

G2.2: The educational system should provide for all people of all ages useful and attractive programmes of learning aimed at developing and up-dating professional/work skills and at affording the widest possible range of opportunities for self-actualisation. Within all educational programmes provision should be made for learners to negotiate their particular needs and to evaluate their own progress and future potential.

G2.3: In a modern, technological society, subject to the pressures of constant change, lifelong education is essential not only to enable individuals to cope with the increasing complexities of everyday life, but also to enable them to play a full part in helping to determine that society's future.

Recommendations

R2.1: A rationalising of existing provision should be undertaken to create a coherent educational system across all levels and all age groups, more readily available to all; and supported by a network of nationally coordinated educational guidance and counselling services.

R2.2: Each learner should be enabled to participate more in decisions affecting his or her learning.

R2.3: Financial remuneration should be made to registered pupils who, if they had opted out of the education service, would qualify for social benefit.

R2.4: Plans should be made for a substantial expansion at higher education level, giving special attention to students of mature age, and considering a variety of modes of attendance and the length of some courses.

18

R2.5: Up-dating/in-service arrangements should be encapsulated within the daily role as well as in special provisions taking place 'off-the-job'; participation in continuous training will be obligatory in some cases.

R2.6: There should be some form of positive discrimination to redress present resource imbalance based on geographical and/or social factors.

R2.7: Positive steps should be taken to extend the resource-sharing provision between private sponsorship and investment on the one hand and public funds at local and national levels on the other.

THE STAGES OF LIFE

This paper was written by:
Dr Donald Bligh,
    Director Exeter University Teaching Services
Mr Ronald Fell,
    Headmaster Formby High School
Mr Noel Picarda-Kemp,
    Assistant Teacher, The Archbishop Ramsey CE School, London
Miss Julia B. Little,
    Careers and Training Development Analyst, London
Mr Vincent Thompson,
    Assistant Director Council for Educational Technology, London

under the chairmanship of:
Miss Diana Whittingham,
    Career Development Consultant, GHN Partners Ltd, London

Hypotheses and their discussions

H3.1: Survival as an adult in the changing, unstable environment of the twenty-first century will require greater maturity, based upon a secure understanding of self, others and an awareness of one's place within the universe. Whatever educational systems exist, they will play a critical part in engendering this sense of personal value and inner resilience.

D3.1: Traditionally permanent family relationships are tending to become temporary, as indeed are the contracts between employee and employer. The increasing intrusion of mass media into the display of private and uncontrolled areas of personal behaviour (e.g. sexual and violent behaviour) has distorted the balance between self and image of

20

self; between personal and vicarious experience; fact and fiction; fantasy and reality.

The sexual identity of men and women and their relationships with each other at work and at home are undergoing profound changes. In some instances, the need to establish sexual equality has led to suppression or denial of any feminine identity. Many women now have the opportunity to combine marriage, motherhood, full-time or part-time work and outside interests; these choices have to be managed. They also have to have regard to their obligations to their marriage partner.

The effect of population growth on the freedom of the individual (e.g. pressures on housing) has resulted in curtailment of many former areas of choice, rigid educational systems and the increase of legislation.

Picking personal paths through complicated and sophisticated systems and organisations is daunting. The increased authority of the 'expert' has led ordinary people to feel that they are no longer in a position to make sense of their surroundings, or come to competent decisions by themselves at any stage of their lives.

People are searching for a pattern and a system of values in life. During this search there is a need for help in reaching self-understanding in questioning prejudices, seeking new directions and focussing on talents.

Education extends formally and informally through the whole of life in helping the child, young adolescent and adult to reach a secure knowledge of themselves and others and to satisfy the inner needs. The whole child goes to school, not just his brain and his body. A whole person needs to emerge, fed, stimulated and nurtured on every level. Inner enrichment is an 'across the curriculum' subject. The disturbing rise in attempted suicide, nervous breakdown, behavioural disorder, and serious illness in children whilst at school gives grave cause for concern. Many leave education unskilled for any employment—many are also leaving unfitted for life itself.

Formidable demands from technology require high levels of pupil competence. More demands are made by the increased quantities of information which have to be absorbed, by the shortage of teaching staff and by earlier sexual maturity. These cause profound upheavals at a time of diminishing resources and rising unemployment.

In terms of guidance about work choices and vocational help, efforts are centred on satisfying needs for immediate jobs. Tackling deeper issues takes time and perseverance, and will not receive immediate answers. Teachers, family, friends, employers are all instrumental in passing on their advice and experience. They can only help with the process of self-understanding if they have come to some point of rest about

21

themselves. Careers education, employer visits and occupational choice are affected by far deeper fears, emotions, ambitions and needs than is commonly recognised.

Future career satisfaction will have to lie not in the job itself but the way it is tackled. However monotonous the work, it has to be turned into some kind of self-expression. In this sense 'vocational education' is feeling its way into the twenty-first century just as people are—conscious of the fact that 'career' no longer means forty years in the same organisation.

If people are to achieve satisfaction they need to understand that there is another, parallel 'career'. It is an inner and personal journey through life. They must learn the need for wonder, they must search for truth, interpret right and wrong, develop a capacity for belief and a sense of their place in the universe. Once established, this vision of oneself, this 'other career', can never be taken away.

The dominance of rational thought, academic prowess, hierarchic achievement has tended to undermine and devalue the other dimensions of life. Young people see themselves as successes or failures, inferior or superior according to their employment prospects.

Increasingly the education process has withdrawn from debating or teaching philosophical issues and values—except in intellectual terms. Teachers and parents, employers and counsellors, social workers and the media all need to respect the inner life needs of the 'other career'. If this challenge is not accepted now, AD 2000 will be the start of a century of bleak idleness or monotonous drudgery for the majority.

H3.2: It will be widely recognised that children's needs and development start at conception; the satisfying of these needs is fundamental to the future self-identity and self-fulfilment.

D3.2: The time from conception to the beginning of compulsory education periods is already accepted as one of great potential development. This is the time when not only the crucial sensory, physical, language and emotional foundations are laid but also marks the beginning of many coordinating activities. These form the basis for coherance as an adult; that is, distinctions between fantasy and reality, apprehension of life and death, a sense of wonder and curiosity about the unknown world as well as security within known family relationships.

In educational terms this is a time when essential skills for life are laid down: in practical areas such as manual dexterity and mental and physical coordination; in intellectual areas such as methods of thought, memory,

22

concentration, imagination; and in the inner areas of identity, capacity for belief, desire for truth, confidence in taking personal risks etc.

The natural focus for all these developments is the home. The parents' role, especially the mother's, is critical at this stage, providing a storehouse of behavioural examples which will be drawn on throughout adulthood. At this moment in life, each imprinted image of experience provides the source of inspiration for future visions and patterns of self-understanding.

Unfortunately, pressures intrude at all social and economic levels of this phase: poor housing, working mothers, single-parent families, anxieties and frustration about external conditions and future prospects rebound on behaviour at home; small families reduce the networks of caring relationships and the range of learning experiences available within the home; lack of community spirit leads to isolation and dependence on experience and stimulation such as that provided by the media which otherwise could be complementary to personal discovery. Poor diet and environmental conditions undermine development and reinforce other problems of health, behaviour and insecurity. Wealthy parents are often too busy with work and social commitments to devote sufficient personal care to their children. Parents of the disabled and handicapped receive insufficient practical and financial help.

Inadequate provisions for existing 'pre-school education' and other state support systems—for example, home-visiting, creches, parental guidance, child care facilities—mean that compensatory support is least available where it is most needed; children enter compulsory education having received widely differing pre-school experiences. The reluctant conclusion has to be drawn that in terms of priority young children in our society receive insufficient government support and finance.

The above review posits a need to give the highest priority to these early years, either by means of re-allocating existing resources to younger age-groups, and/or by encouraging the creation of low-cost schemes and networks, which can operate in a flexible manner through small groups to fit the various social needs and working patterns of future family life. These support systems should be freely available to all families with young children, regardless of income group, race, colour or creed, so that every child faces an equal chance of reaching its full potential in human terms.

Whatever facilities are set up—whether playgroups, nurseries, creches, home-visits or other networks—they should all be based on creating and enhancing a close and stable fabric of relationships centred on the home. This is the forum for creating an integrated sense of personal identity

23

which can form coherence out of future conflicting aspirations, pressures and adult life systems.

Finally, problems of young inexperienced parents, single-parents and those with special difficulties such as caring for handicapped children, as well as those with differing cultural backgrounds and traditional customs, must be taken into account, and catered for together with and not separately from others. Somehow the cycle of deprivation has to be broken without creating further, remote, costly and bureaucratic structures. These lead to further deprivations being created, removing the caring role to yet another outside 'agent' or 'expert', and inestimable costs in terms of further remedial help.

If the twenty-first century is to differ fundamentally from those that have preceeded it, it has to begin in the nurturing of gentleness and care from the moment of new life.

H3.3: Children differ; the family, educational establishments and the community all have a part to play in children's development. The provision for children's needs must be flexible in order to prepare them for life in the twenty-first century.

D3.3: Children differ in colour, height, weight, social competence, intelligence, etc. Insufficient regard is given to individual differences, especially during formal schooling.

We do not fully understand how children learn other than there are different routes to learning. Our ignorance in this matter places them at risk.

It is vital to recognise individual differences and stages of development and contracts between teacher and taught should consider factors as follows:

(a)   sex and ethnic needs, e.g. during puberty, language problems;
(b)   the variety of learning experiences used;
(c)   groupings of children;
(d)   appropriate styles of learning/teaching.

It should be accepted that no single type of educational institution is capable of catering for these differences. Our general expectations of what school will provide are too broad and make impossible demands on the school. Learning takes place in all aspects of life.

The influence of the home should be recognised far more. There children learn social values, but the new technology (e.g. Prestel, cable TV) and the new methodologies of 'distance learning' (e.g. the Open University)

24

will enable a home of the future to become an intellectual place of learning.

New technology should be seen as being complementary and not an alternative to fundamental learning processes such as memory, methods of thinking, etc. We need to distinguish clearly between an awareness of how to use technology in order to enhance learning opportunities and what the curriculum need is to introduce an awareness of the use of technology throughout life.

New forms of technology and technological processes will supplement—not replace—the work of schools. However, a reappraisal of the role of schools will be essential especially in the light of the differing roles teachers will play. Their new role will cover a variety of professional skills.

Parents will be encouraged to participate more willingly in the education of their children. They may receive through this involvement further motivation to quench their own latent thirst for further education.

Schools will become community education centres supporting individuals and groups. They will also provide counselling and consultant services, e.g. vocational/careers guidance, help with independent study, as well as being more widely used throughout each day and at weekends. This practice is already being developed in Leicestershire and Cambridgeshire.

Each educational centre would require a new role; that of developing community activities which would encourage children and adults to join in activities together. This will provide a new breadth to the curriculum. Talents and abilities, hitherto unused, will be used to supplement the teacher's professional competencies. The introduction of technology will also support a shift of power from teacher to learner and create a demand for a rationalisation of syllabus and the re-organisation of the timetable.

A new broad-based, non-specialist concept of *basic* education and *post-basic* education (see appendix) will be called for. Students will receive a foundation education up to 14 years, thereafter they will receive, as of right, a further 7 years of post-basic education, as and when they perceive their individual needs for it. They will be encouraged, however, to fulfil their own potential at an early age in whatever direction their talents lie.

In basic education the family will play a more significant role by extending its function throughout the local community. The family will be supported by home tutors, community counsellors and newly emerging professional and non-professional groups.

Relationships which have suffered through the effects of large schools will be reintegrated by the establishment of smaller networks of relationships built up around the family and local community instead of reliance upon outside advice and experience.

Greater emphasis in education centres will be placed upon life-preparation courses. These will be set in relevant cultural contexts, viz.:

(a)   survival skills (see appendix);
(b)   counselling (personal, vocational, etc.);
(c)   life skills (see appendix);
(d)   education for parenthood/citizenship;
(e)   education in social and political processes;
(f)   health education;
(g)   a basic legal education;
(h)   leisure and recreational pursuits;
(i)   learning skills;

N.B. These topics should not be seen as independent but interrelated.

This wider curriculum will be the means whereby we assist individual development. Its aim must be the enrichment of the whole person, and the focussing on their particular strengths will ensure that developing their potential is success in its own right.

The role of the community is vital—it must be fully involved; provide leadership, ideas, and finance; provide security and effect the development of relationships. Industry and commerce must participate in the 'secret garden' and thus sow the seeds of communal harmony.

No longer will the teaching profession be observed as the only 'teachers' in these new educational centres. Their skills will enable them to lead the new ancilliary forces. Each person will have an indirect 'teaching' obligation towards young people whenever we are in contact with each other. Young people, too, have much to contribute to adults, and particularly to the elderly.

Such a stance will provide teachers with greater status. However, their training and background should reflect wider life experiences than at present. The system encourages insularity of the individual teacher and school. The way for them to acquire these experiences must be viewed as a matter of urgent priority. They should be encouraged, for instance, into other types of employment for short periods, for example, in commerce or industry.

This new teaching force will provide a mix of people who will be in a better position to close generation gaps. This will enable us jointly to reduce social disorders, violence and vandalism by better relationships and agreed actions.

Learning will be provided at a variety of levels equal in status. Facilities will be opened to all. Retraining, in-service training, refresher and enrichment courses will coexist with basic skills in education centres. This will enable women returning to work, unemployed fathers and young people to learn the same skills side-by-side.

Flexibility will be vital and include vertical grouping, joint child/adult teaching; shared and group learning as well as independent study.

The present examination system is an educational straitjacket and new forms of assessment should include a system of 'profiling' which describes the satisfaction of individual or group needs, personal competencies and attitudes. In this way the individual as a whole may be perceived positively by himself and others.

This system should be based upon the redistribution of existing resources. It may well cost less because community self-help in fund-raising will be encouraged.

Such a system, based upon perceived individual needs and stages of development, will strengthen the nation at a time of exponential change. Its strength will be its ability to react immediately to such change.

H3.4: Because of cumulative changes in society generally, young adults will be faced with and will need wide experience and experimentation. This will be in forms of work, leisure, education and personal relationships.

D3.4: The stage of early adulthood is a time of experimentation in relationships and of struggling to find an identity. Young people want to try out this emerging personality in a variety of groupings. Financial constraints and lack of status in the community can make this an empty and frustrating time. In search of support they seek stable friendships. Early marriage—risky at best—is often embarked upon to satisfy very urgent needs for mutual support.

The clannish nature of young people, their dress, and the behavioural fashions of a number of them, frequently alienate the community. They in turn tend to reject former support groups. The lounger can move from street corner to public house. An element are attracted to hooliganism and crime to escape from monotony. The need to experiment can develop into an interest in politics, religion, cults or spectator sports which provide the feeling of group belonging. The generation gap and need for independence can lead to separation from the family and adult friends. In extreme forms gang life, sexual aberration, drink, drugs and car thefts can damage their long-term status in the community. The police and social workers join teachers as 'them' and the new peer group is 'us'. Boys are ridiculed for wanting to enter 'caring' professions and girls can be mocked if they aspire to apprenticeships in traditionally male-dominated industries.

The present situation in education has led to narrow subject options, early specialisation and crucial choices between leaving school or staying on, studying arts or sciences, further study or seeking work. What is needed is a broad base from which further choices can be made both in educational and in occupational terms.

This needs to be a time of experimentation. For girls, this is the make-or-break time in working life; *if* they leave school with the 'right' subjects; *if* they are not sucked into routine clerical work; *if* their school and home life has encouraged them to think beyond tomorrow; *if* they have been given confidence to make mistakes and try things out, they will stand a good chance of establishing an autonomous working life. The penalty for not doing so is monotony, restricted choice, staying below the dividing line between jobs with challenge and those with none. The same applies to men.

The work jungle has its own tribal laws and these will increase as competition for fewer jobs gets keener: no jobs without job experience and no part-time work without previous full-time work. The unwritten laws on how to behave at interviews, fill in application forms and present the right pieces of paper in order to find right of entry, will become even more important. The real problem in the twenty-first century will be that there will *always* be enough talented, articulate, confident, experienced, ready-made people. Employers won't want to dissipate their energies any more on less able people who are unlikely to find employment anywhere. For the lucky ones who enter large corporation life, the jungle will get more impenetrable except for the very few who come in destined for stardom. Women often need a crash course in confidence-building, organisation map-reading and making themselves visible within an amorphous organisation.

All this folk-lore has to be learned quickly in order to create a platform for personal change and later re-direction. Women will want to be able to leave work and have the chance to return without playing snakes-and-ladders with their qualifications and experience. To do this they have to manoeuvre their way into acquiring experience and qualifications which are viewed to be 'useful'.

The world of tertiary education and study has become another jungle. Options, units, entry-levels, modules, exemptions and clearing-houses have all sprung up like creepers choking off or entangling all but the most sophisticated. It is now quite impossible to take full advantage of tertiary education without 'expert' help. There is a great need for simplification. The opportunities in education are useless if they are not known to be there by ordinary people.

It is useless to talk in terms of mobility of the labour-force, retraining for new careers, making the most of opportunites, if no back-up advice is provided. As a result the consequences of vital personal decisions

28

concerning work cannot be fully debated. At present many young people are being launched on the path to certain crisis.

> **H3.5: For many, the years between late twenties and mid forties will be the most fulfilling period of their life.**
> **But for an increasing number, it will be a time of blocked careers or joblessness. Unless a reappraisal of the work ethic takes place, this will lead to alienating frustration.**

D3.5: By the beginning of the twenty-first century, the pattern of working life for those in their twenties to forties will be greatly different from now. For many, this will mean long periods without work. For those who are working, working from home, flexible working hours, sabbatical leave, job-sharing, part-time, secondment and lateral moves between the various employment sectors will all be commonplace.

The relationship between employer and employee will undergo further changes, with increasing transfer of pension rights. This will enable short-term contracts, retainer schemes, consultant status and self-employment to form part of many people's career progression. Since few people will stay in one organisation for all their working life, the conflicts will increasingly lie in the division between jobs which, possibly circum-scribed by new technology, are routine, and those which have room for judgement, decision-taking, expansion of responsibilty and initiative. For many people a 'career' between late twenties and forties will mean making their current job more interesting and challenging, moving 'sideways' into other jobs at the same level and turning more attention to outside interests. Others who have hitherto been blocked in jobs with little room for autonomy, the gateway to achieving future greater self-determination and respect at work is access to an education system adapted to fit the future patterns of employment and family life. The traditional concept of long courses on single subjects is already giving way to shorter courses with many different patterns of instruction, attendance and learning methods. This is beginning to answer the problems of employees reluctant to jeopardise job security for the sake of retraining, employers unable to spare people from jobs for long periods, rapid changes in information and the high costs of 'residential' courses.

This is important in all sectors of employment, including that of education and teacher training itself, where the need for updating and refreshment is vital. There is indeed a move towards suggesting that those with any 'professional' status or qualifications should be periodically required to update their skills and refresh their energies; particular attention must be given to the reductions of demands in stressful occupations.

At the same time, when energy levels are high, so are the demands made upon them. Some occupations or levels of job responsibility will demand more stamina than others, leaving more or less energy for outside interests and family commitments. The effects of marriage, late child-bearing, ageing parents, young children with both partners working, will be to place increasing strain on the stability of these relationships. This will often lead to considerable re-appraisal and change of attitude. Many forms of advice and help are needed. This is not the perogative of so-called experts. Thus where it appears that no help is at present available, properly pointed, existing resources can be coordinated to fill the gap.

This can also be a highly 'mobile' stage in life where people can prepare themselves for future alternatives in life-style. Sufficient experience and confidence may have now been gained to consider the possibilities of creating new interests, hobbies and businesses as a supplement to their present life and provide an escape route for the future. This is of particular significance to women wanting to create a worthwhile purpose to their lives through work or leisure.

If the educational system is sufficiently responsive, no separate major requirements or expenditure should be necessary. Adults of all ages should be able to share and cooperate in mutual support—for example, the redundant executive, the mother returning to work and the individual looking for new directions. Such courses as are available should contain elements which will permit credit transfer of skills and qualifications. The idea that there is a fixed path to happiness and knowledge needs to be rejected.

If the above is to be achieved, employers must be prepared to invest in these mutual needs to determine life patterns, so that early retirement is a much more realisable aim and less threatening prospect for both parties. The costs and benefits of this investment will be a national one.

Realising these potentialities will require major changes in attitudes towards employment, including a re-appraisal of the status of particular careers and jobs, for example those of teachers.

H3.6: All employed or unemployed people in their forties to sixties will inevitably face some major problems and decisions which will provoke fundamental self re-appraisal.

D3.6: There are many who are satisfied with the type of work they do and feel they have reached an acceptable level of responsibility;

this group may even include some whose careers have not advanced in line with their original aspirations. For these people the final period of working life will be one of contentment.

As children grow up, pressures on family relations should reduce, and the lessening strain of financial resources will in many cases coincide with increases in income exceeding or at least in line with inflation. Reduction in the length of working days will result in new forms of cultural and intellectual leisure interests or of recreation.

There will be opportunities for recreation and travel, for making use of local educational facilities and playing a more active part in the local community. Housewives, freed from child-rearing responsibilities, will be able to devote more time to paid or voluntary work, leisure activities and travel.

Some people will prepare positively for their retirement years, planning their financial affairs and structuring their lives in anticipation of inevitable changes. Others, however, will be unprepared and will face a major personal crisis which some will not survive.

One traumatic and likely crisis now and in the future is the loss of a job. For some in the later years of their working lives this may well be a job which they held for considerable time so that the shock to them is extreme. Steps must be taken to minimise the impact of this by the need to acquire new skills. Ideally this should be done in advance of the threatening situation as part of a personal survival strategy. Career counselling should be provided within and without the place of employment and available at all levels of job seniority. The result could be an ability to operate on a self-employed basis, providing advisory or manual services alone or with a small workforce. Educational centres should be encouraged and enabled to provide additional relevant training and supplement courses available largely within professional and management institutions.

It should be possible for the years of accumulated experience in one type of employment to be applied elsewhere. A business executive working on a part-time and/or a short-term basis can impart invaluable knowledge to students financing their career plans. There are great advantages in transfers of individuals between the different working sectors (educational, commerce, private and public industries etc.). Such transfers enhance the knowledge and understanding of the groups concerned. The opportunity to gain new knowledge may compensate for the fact that such transfers will not always fully reflect the responsibilities previously held.

There is evidence today that increasing numbers of people seek or are reconciled to giving up work before their normal retirement age. Employers are offering 'early retirment' arrangements to people at all levels. Because of the present pensions scheme limitations, not everyone receives an adequate pension and the early leaver can be seriously penalised. Some people decide not to seek similar employment; instead they 'opt out' of the system, expecting to be able to survive financially, possibily with state assistance. They hope to supplement their drastically reduced employment pension by an occasional payment for some type of work. These aspire to a free life-style, relieved of the stresses and demands of working life. It seems inevitable that this action will be taken by more and more people in the future.

Another extreme shock faced by many in their forties and fifties is that which follows the death of husband or wife. Apart from sheer loneliness and the fear of being unwanted, many widows and widowers need to learn practical budgeting and housekeeping skills not previously encountered, for which they are educationally ill-equipped.

Educational establishments provide training by access to some facilities usually at evening classes. There is a need for day classes for people who are not employed or who are reluctant to travel alone in the evening. Concentrated courses, residential or non-residential, should be offered. These accelerate the learning process and provide experience sharing opportunities exceeding the usual weekly one- or two-hour arrangements. Whilst the subjects studied are important, often the major benefit results from the building of friendships and the sharing of experience.

The impact of personal crises that so often occur in middle life can be reduced by sensible preparation by individuals, with specialised and general help from the community. The transition to active retirement should be a smooth and welcomed one.

H3.7: Society will adopt a much more positive approach to the years of formal retirement. It will be an active period in which people will continue their learning and contribute their wisdom to the family and the community.

D3.7: The elderly should properly be regarded as a valuable asset of the community. It is present practice to regard them as a burden upon both the family and the community. Government policies reflect this premise. The rapidly growing size of the post-retirement age group is regarded as a problem requiring increasing resources.

At present society perceives old age as consisting of two distinct periods. Where the elderly live in the community, they have a 'grandparental' role, both in and out of the family. With deterioration of physical and mental health, they move to a secondary stage. Here they are seen by the family,

32

community, and themselves as a 'burden'. This stage will absorb an ever increasing amount of financial and support services.

In the previous comments of this chapter the role that the elderly can play in the whole system of education has been indicated. Reciprocally those responsible for children's learning should educate them for gentleness, particularly towards the elderly. This education needs to embrace hitherto taboo subjects such as death, old age, and infirmity. Violence towards the elderly will decline if the young have close association with the old.

Many children run errands and perform tasks for elderly relatives or neighbours. There should be a constant effort to foster in children this care of the old.

The physical and mental problems of old age must be more generally alleviated by community involvement.

Schools, in their new role as education for life centres, are in an ideal position to help the young, the recently retired, those between education and work, or those between jobs, to be involved in this supportive process.

The young should assist the elderly to shop, maintain their homes, and to enjoy exercise and recreation. This will provide the opportunity for those of different generations to benefit from the experience and wisdom of the old and the enthusiasm and curiosity of the young.

Education centres should help both pupils and members of the old overcome or cope with their infirmities. Additionally help could be given to assist them to understand and react to modern legislation, for example, form-filling, tax returns etc. They must not be seen as recipients of blanket provisions of private charity. Prolonged independence must be the goal.

Existing networks in the community can be utilised to identify old people at the risk of being isolated and in the bringing of resources to the elderly. The postman, the milkman and the good neighbour already assume these roles.

All the skills exist to mitigate the problems of old age within the community. The recognition of the benefits to both the elderly and the younger generations implicit in strengthening existing support will provide the impetus for the considerable advance in this area in the short- and medium-term.

Special points

S3.1: Teachers will have an enhanced value and require highly developed talents to service the education of the community in the future. If education is going to develop the potential of every citizen, the teacher will need prior experience gained in the workaday world. They should not have to leave the classroom to seek promotion in pastoral or administration posts. Ancilliary provision and higher financial rewards for good practice will give successful teachers the status they deserve. Continuing in-service training and attendance at refreshment courses will develop their professional skills; lateral movement to and from the civil service and other forms of employment will add to their experiences and is to be encouraged. The implications for the selection procedures, training, assessment and further development of teachers are therefore considerable.

S3.2: Some of the problems experienced particularly by people in their mid or late employment periods will not be alleviated until the government in practical terms supports the concept of easier labour mobility. This must include means of transferance by council tenants to rented property in other local councils; increased transferability of pensions across the various employer groups; and removal of early leaver pension penalties.

S3.3: The role of careers education within schools and other agencies involved must be recreated and coordinated to reflect that careers choice is a decision made as a result of structured and unstructured influences upon the individual, that is to say:
(a)   home conditions and family opinions;
(b)   active tutorial and pastoral learning;
(c)   the influence of visiting employers, recruitment officers;
(d)   visits to potential employers;
(e)   work experience while at school;
(f)   general education/life skills education;
(g)   specific career teaching;
(h)   the decision to seek further or higher education.
        Teachers' counsellors and potential employers should be familiar
        with the various needs discerned by the individual.
Courses, profiles, and certification will reflect and record the acquisition of skills and preparation for employment, self-employment, further study or a constructive use of enforced leisure.
Counselling at this period should build upon previous education to help the client:
(a)   select from a realistic cross-section of potential employment
        opportunity;
(b)   bear in mind the need to acquire more training where appropriate;

(c)   face up to the possibility of the unexpected loss of that job through no fault of either employer or employee;

(d)   appreciate that career prospects may fail to reach the client's expectations;

(e)   accept that there will be continuing need to make the best opportunity of career counselling throughout their chosen careers;

(f)   understand that where expectations are not fulfilled, such counselling together with training and the support of parents and friends can help cushion the shock; and

(g)   help in the search for alternative paid employment or retraining.

This will entail a much closer cooperation between all education centres and counselling agencies and a thorough understanding by them of the methods used and contents of the forms of education with which they, the pupil and later the mature person, are familiar.

Where such liaison or skills do not exist, special counselling skills will be needed especially during the short- and medium-term implementation of these proposals.

Recommendations

R3.1: *To the Prime Minister:* There should be an immediate reallocation of resources and cooperation between local, national and voluntary services to make provision for all children to enjoy educational stimulation before they are deemed to have reached the age for compulsory education (LEA).

R3.2: The training and rewards of those working with pre-school children should be enhanced and a greater number of male teachers should be encouraged to enter this field (LEA).

R3.3: Future educational systems should take more account of children's individual differences and development and compulsory education should consist of two stages:

1   basic (up to 14 years);

2   a further 7 years of post-basic education will be a universal right (DES).

R3.4: There should be greater devolution of resources in education direct to local communities under the guidance of central government. Community education centres should be established (DES).

R3.5: Careers services should be encouraged and extended. They should include adults as a matter of urgency (government, LEAs).

R3.6: The appropriate bodies should be encouraged to provide more short occupationally-related courses with open access. Support services to such initiatives will be required (NAB).

R3.7: In all types of employment, opportunities should be provided for updating or retraining their skills and refreshing themselves, on a full- or part-time basis (public/private sector, industry, commerce).

R3.8: The young should be encouraged for their own educational development in the community to join in the care of the elderly (school, LEAs, social services).

Appendix
Life skills—forms basic for profiling:
    Money management
    Developing and sustaining relationships
    Understanding of self
    Risk-taking and desision-making
    Value systems, morality, religion
    Reasoning
    Social skills
    Inventive skills—creativity
    Manual dexterity
    Leadership—cooperation
    Oral communication
    Self-discipline
    Memory training—concentration—application
    Methods of problem-solving
    Spiritual values—capacity for belief—wonder
    Psycho-motor skills
    Persistance—tolerance
    Self-reliance
    Flexibility
  This is not an exclusive list!

EDUCATION, SKILL AND CHANGE

This paper was written by:
Mr Anthony Lewis,
  Manager-Education and Training, Ford Motor Company
Mrs Pauline Russack,
  Student in Adult Education
The Revd J. Felix Stephens OSB,
  Housemaster, Ampleforth College, York
Major General H. G. Woods CB,
  Head of CIEL (West and North Yorkshire)
Mr John D. Wymer,
  London

under the chairmanship of:
Dr John G. Axford,
  Manager Education and Scientific Programmes, IBM

Hypotheses and their discussions

H4.1: The aims of education should not be subject to pre-determined limits, but should allow people to exceed rather than to be constrained by their supposed capabilities.

D4.1: First, we believe in seeking after the best—the best that teachers can provide, the best skills that can be achieved by the pupil. The best is always a goal to be striven for: objectively, it may result in mediocrity; but for the teacher or pupil it is the fulfilment of individual expertise and talent.

We reject the relativist position which seeks to educate to a level of acceptable norms, reasonably attainable, but which do not challenge the individual either by their demands or because of the sameness of the standard which results.

Second, we believe that in each individual there is a yearning to seek

37

and strive after something beyond the mundane, the ordinary and even the worldly. To some it goes by the name faith; to others, excellence; to others it remains a confused search for self identity.

In educational terms it is a combination of factors, not all of which are perceived by any particular individual: the drawing out of the creative power of man; the releasing of the imagination of man, in seeking to master the world about him; the search for absolute moral standards to which to aspire; the search for belief in a power outside man; belief and practice of a religious faith.

Third, this search and idealism among the young is balanced by potential for judgement. The educational system should draw out the native and often earthy common sense of the young, but it can only be achieved if these are worth striving for: things which require the acceptance of disciplines in order to discover freedom; effort and concentration in the acquiring of knowledge and skills; and perseverance in striving to apply them without loss of enthusiasm under trial or failure.

A failure to set high standards of discipline, morality and teaching will result in disillusionment with what is on offer, and in consequence a youth sub-culture, naive yet honest, prone to excess in the highs of drugs or mass hysteria, and the lows of rejection and violence.

In short, the young should be presented with challenges, so as to assess their own capacities and to judge their actions accordingly. Life will treat many of them hard and they need all the inner strengths we can give them, if they are to become resilient and balanced in their judgement.

Fourth, the sheer pace of technological advance today necessitates change to which the world of education must respond courageously and creatively. Every generation has complained about the difficulty of coming to terms with the speed of change and the uncertainty of the future. Rapid change can be a recipe for instability; but we foresee a world of increasingly rapid change. We need therefore to ensure that the actual process of change is constructive and not disruptive.

At any given moment of educational change, a generation of children is being educated. And we know that their upbringing and education requires the right blend of certitude and flexibility. In short, and put negatively, we must never destroy what is excellent in order to make room for something new and untested; equally what is new and judged to be essential must be incorporated into an existing system, even if existing excellence is forced to adapt and change to new circumstances.

Finally, there is the self-educating influence of the peer group of young people. By this is meant any group of the young whose presence, power for good or ill, group behaviour and culture, is all the greater as a group than the sum of its parts. The adult likes to think he or she relates to this peer group and can influence it. In reality this is not so. The group influence is self-generating and develops the attitudes and outlook of the next generation. And the group has its leader, because it is the nature of the young to group behind a leader.

The role of parent and teacher of the individual young is to lead and guide unashamedly and with conviction. If the leadership is sound and of good judgement, firm and yet able to carry others along, then the peer group is respectful of the leadership, embraces the standards offered, and reacts accordingly but in its own language. There is no substitute for leadership.

H4.2: Education for Capability: we should strive for the application of creativity and knowledge into practical skills.

D4.2: Skill is needed to create wealth. Wealth is needed to sustain our society.

Greater emphasis will be placed on skill capability in education. We endorse one initiative in particular—the Education for Capability project sponsored by the Royal Society of Arts and supported by leading academics and industrialists. The aim is to make education more focussed on enabling people of all ages to transfer creativity and knowledge into practical action.

In supporting these moves, we do not deny the value of the academic side of education. This allows appreciation of and fulfilment in the liberal arts and the natural world. This side of education must be available for everyone.

Neither do we deny that there is much education which *is* directed towards specific skills, both within and without the curriculum.

But in the area of general education the balance is wrong—too much inappropriate knowledge and not enough skill is being taught to meet the demands of modern adult life. Of those skill initiatives which do exist, most are not integrated in the curriculum, few are examined, and all are virtually absent from formal qualifications.

There are three reasons for this imbalance.

First, the university dominance of the examination system. We do not deny the value of an academic career path, but we need to ask: Why should the agency which accepts about 10 per cent of the school output effectively determine the measurement apparatus for the other 90 per cent? Why should the same agency set its own measurement standards when by and large it is not its own customer? Why should some 40 per cent of the school output be deprived of any meaningful measurement at all?

Second, the status of academic achievement. We are a curious society that strives after a form of achievement which is of minimal relevance to most of us. This distortion of educational value leads to a sense of failure which destroys incentive to achieve in other directions.

Third, the difficulty of measuring skills. Skill attainment is not as easy to measure as knowledge, especially for the more complex skills acquired as we grow older. For instance, it is easier to measure skill in reading at five years, than skill in literary criticism at twenty.

The solutions to these problems are not easy to see, and education alone cannot be blamed for them; industry and government must take their share of responsibility.

What are the particular skills where the greatest need lies? First, there are technical skills necessary for wealth creation. In some areas these are well catered for, such as in education for the practising professions. In others, such as general science and engineering, more can be done to improve the practical capability of the graduate, both from school and college.

It cannot be too strongly emphasised that a very large increase in the number and status of competent engineering and science practitioners is vital to the maintenance of the UK economy.

But there are in addition 'life' skills, education for which should, as of right, be available to all who pass through the educational system. They provide an essential tool-kit for life fulfilment and for contributing to society. Examples, with no claim to completeness, are:
- to be competent and responsible parents;
- to be able to communicate;
- to be able to adapt;
- to handle complexity;
- to undertake enterprise;
- to use leisure.

We might add to this list capabilities which at first sight appear more to do with attitudes than skill, but are nevertheless needed for the continuance of a stable society, such as:
- to exercise a willingness to contribute to society;
- to work cooperatively with others;
- to adopt a tolerant, constructive approach to others in a multi-racial, multi-sectarian society.

40

H4.3: Curriculum: pragmatic flexibility will operate in an era of accelerating technological change.

D4.3: In this discussion, we only intend to emphasise the importance of incorporating technology as a normal part of the curriculum for every pupil.

A generation gap exists in the language and content of technology, between the teacher, trained as a child of his time, and the pupil at ease with the products of the ever-changing microchip revolution. We must harness the natural desire of the young to understand and live with technological change by using technology as a means of encouraging the natural skills of the young.

This process will involve intellectually demanding skills: the ability to identify, examine and solve problems, use a variety of materials, and in so doing stretch to the full the pupil's inventive and innovatory powers. The pupil thereby acquires the capability to synthesise these skills into the successful solution to a practical design problem.

This needs to be developed, re-assessed and integrated into the mainstream of educational process. A start has been made in the current discipline of craft, design and technology.

Industrial change is linked with social change. New technologies and the reduction of levels and hours of employment give rise to new needs: industrial, individual, and social. The educational curriculum must make its contribution to be abreast of and even ahead of its time in shaping the future.

There is one other aspect of the curriculum which needs to be kept at the forefront of thinking about educational change: the role of history. A sense of history means the placing of a child's life in the context of historical change. We realise the pitfalls inherent in historical interpretation. Nevertheless, we believe that history and related disciplines provide a necessary perspective which assists the young in understanding the context within which their lives are to be lived, including the advance of technology.

H4.4: The good teacher remains the central influence, aided by the use of technology.

D4.4: The educational system requires those responsible for sustaining and developing it to be at the forefront of change.

The ability to respond to this challenge will be the criterion by which all sections of society will be judged. The influence of 'the good teacher' is paramount as the process of change accelerates and more is demanded of the system.

Teachers are expected to be dedicated and enthusiastic, seeking through instruction, discussion and example to impart knowledge and skill to stimulate and influence the development of their pupils. In the ferment of continuous change, they will need all the support that society and technology can provide.

All aspects of the educational system will be changed, for example:

–   quality;
–   the curriculum;
–   measures of achievement.

Too often we emphasise failure. The growth of learning should be accompanied by a system of assessment which should always be constructive, continuous, and result in the fulfilment of individual potential.

The resources of the teacher should be continuously re-assessed in the light of the growth of knowledge and the acceptance that certain areas of knowledge, both analytical and practical, can become redundant.

In the light of the above, selection criteria should be re-examined. This must be carried out professionally and involve all sectors of society. Similarly, the selection process itself should be participative. Such a process of involvement will widen the influence of teachers through the broader allocation and acceptance of responsibility for selection.

It will be against this background of professional, participative selection, and continuous examination of the relevance and balance of knowledge and skill, that both initial and in-service training will be undertaken.

Teachers will realise their obligation to be up to date.

In this context, technology must support and not supplant.

It can take over from the teachers many of those areas which take up teaching time. The learning process can be extended through the use of communications technology, for example:

–   inter-active distance learning;
–   access to large and diverse data bases;
–   video conferencing;
–   many others as yet undreamt of.

Coordinated and professional studies involving teachers, designers and developers of relevant technology need to ensure that advantage is taken of opportunities for improvement.

There will be as professional an approach to technology as to any other area of knowledge and skill. Its understanding and use will ensure that teachers retain the initiative, thereby minimising the de-humanising effects of alternative, wholly technologically based systems.

The teacher will also benefit from the use of technology in improving educational management and administration.

H4.5: The partnership between the education and wealth-creation sectors will be an integral part of the education process.

D4.5: The wealth-creation sector should recognise its fundamental obligation to be an active partner in the educational process far beyond a mere contribution through taxes.

Partnership between the education and wealth-creation sectors will become much more effective by AD 2000, at least to the extent already achieved in Europe, Japan, and North America. At present there is a failure to achieve full inter-communication or effective and widespread understanding on both sides. Moreover, society fails to value, in the right proportion, the intellectual abilities and practical achievement.

The examination system, effectively determined by the universities, emphasises that achievement is an exclusively academic quality. Consequently, the less able are driven to consider themselves inadequate and failures in life as early as the age of eleven. Often, their achievements after leaving school reveal the potential the educational system should have discovered and nurtured.

Training and education are different, the latter subsuming the former. But the widely held belief that training, unlike education, is intellectually undemanding may be the reason why the educational system fails to emphasise the links between them or the crucial part which training must play in education. We do not exploit, as key elements of both training and education, the importance of accurate and thorough analysis within problem-solving contexts, as for example in design education. When the links between training and education are not explicit, incentives which value educational experiences at school or subsequently are weaker. Students fail to see connections with real life, because the technological environment of such experiences remains largely unperceived. The uninhibited enthusiasm of primary school children for computer-based learning shows what arouses the wish to be educated.

We believe that the partnership must strive to:

- widen understanding of wealth creation, its place in the community, and the encouragement of entrepreneurial skills;
- improve the acceptability of the design and engineering professions and their social dimension through a curriculum which has a practical bias for all levels of ability, and is designed to increase adaptability to the impact of change;

43

— manage a general pattern of continuing and adult education beyond compulsory schooling, which is related to the career patterns and widening responsibilities of those in the wealth-creation sector.

The wealth-creation sector must be a responsible, active and integral part of the process leading to improved and refined methods of measuring achievements, provided that they understand the role of education.

General comments

G4.1: In AD 2000, as now, we are concerned that education should not be undermined with shifting norms and conflicting objectives.

G4.2: The process of education in AD 2000 must be the joint responsibility of the teaching profession, the home, the community and the wealth-creation sector.

G4.3: The teacher (as a person) remains the central influence on the pupil and will not be supplanted by technology. The result is a high professional demand on the role of a teacher.

G4.4: The education measurement system needs a complete overhaul and the examination system must become 'no longer the master but the servant of the curriculum' (quote from the notes accompanying the 1918 Education Act).

Recommendations

R4.1: The curriculum must achieve the right balance between knowledge and skill appropriate to the needs of adult life. The core curriculum must include literacy, numeracy, life skills, and the application of technology.

R4.2: The measurement system should be such that:
— it acknowledges even minimal success;
— the measurement criteria are re-examined.

R4.3: The partnership between the teaching profession and the wealth-creation sector should be intensified:

44

- to enhance mutual understanding;
- to collaborate over curriculum content;
- to create a mutually-beneficial system.

R4.4: The skill and discipline of practical design should be introduced into the curriculum for all children. The details can vary widely, but the creative elements of this discipline should be part of every child's experience and skill.

R4.5: The responsibility for the selection and training of teachers should be extended beyond the profession, and should amongst others include the wealth-creation sector.

R4.6: The in-service training of teachers should be planned, obligatory, and relevant to the changes in society, including technological changes.

R4.7: The use and experience of technology must permeate the whole curriculum.

R4.8: Education, aided by industry and others as appropriate, should develop better ways of measuring skill attainment.

THE SCHOOL AS AN INSTITUTION

This paper was written by:
Sister Mary Francis CRSS,
  Headmistress, New Hall School, Chelmsford
Dr Brian W. Martin,
  Head of English Dept, Magdalen College School,
  Lecturer, Pembroke College, Oxford
Dr W. Bonney Rust OBE,
  Educational Consultant
Mr Nigel G. G. Webb,
  Housemaster and Head of Mathematics,
  Oakham School, Leicestershire
Mrs Susie Wysock-Wright,
  Housewife and Farm Manager, Sussex
Mr Christopher Wysock-Wright,
  Chairman, Wrightson Wood

under the chairmanship of:
Mr Michael N. Duffy,
  Headmaster, King Edward VI School, Morpeth

Hypotheses and their discussions

H5.1: A changed school system will be required in the provision of education to the year 2000 and beyond.

D5.1: We considered the alternatives such as those put forward by advocates of 'deschooling' in the sixties and the more recent idea of home-based learning through modern technological aids but rejected them in favour of a school-based education.

We believe that the financial cost of a school system would be justified by the benefits it can provide for the development of the individual and

46

for society as a whole. We see it as a cost-effective way of providing for education.

A school system can cater for the social development of its pupils by providing:

- a wider range of experience than may be found in the home;
- the opportunity to develop in a structured and ordered environment;
- a framework for learning to live in a pluralist society;
- the opportunity for interaction between pupils and a training in both collaboration and healthy competition.

A school system can lend support to the psychological and moral development of its pupils:

- through pastoral care, by which it may give appropriate support to the family where this is needed;
- through its structured environment by which it can provide a sense of security;
- through pupil-teacher interaction.

Through the school system, pupils have access to the accumulated knowledge, experience and cultural heritage of society by contact with the scholarship and expertise of many teachers and access to a wide range of educational and physical facilities.

A school system can economically provide a range of facilities for the development of the physical, intellectual, practical and aesthetic talents of the pupils.

H5.2: The function of the school system will be to provide:

1 Nursery education for the 3–5 year olds;
2 A general education for all children 5–14;
3 A progressive, credit-earning education for all young people 14–16;
4 A centre for full- or part-time continuing education for students of 16–18 and adults;
5 A focus and a resource for local community education and activity.

D5.2:

1 Nursery provision will benefit:
children, through early access to other children and adults, resources and materials;
parents, who will be freed to pursue other tasks;
society, which will benefit from a more flexible work force.

47

2   The general education from 5 to 14 will provide for the same balance of curriculum for all children, while making provision for a range of age and ability, to equip the children for whatever education and experience follows. The following areas will be included: language and literacy; numbers and mathematics; science and technology; physical and manipulative skills; aesthetic and creative arts; computer skills; religious education; humanities; constructive recreational pursuits and community service. Towards the end of this period, children will be prepared for an element of choice at the next stage and given the opportunity to regard the school increasingly as a learning centre, in which they have some responsibility to initiate learning and choose their activities.

3   The education of the 14–16 group must be based on the achievement of success, not the experience of failure. Its structure should permit the gaining of credit for completed learning units and the transfer to new courses at an appropriate attainment level during this two-year period.

4   By using the school as a centre for continuing education for the 16–18 age group and adults, we believe we shall achieve:
the better use of expensive resources, plant, equipment and teaching expertise, especially if all local schools and FE colleges have access to each other's specialist facilities;
the provision, within a local context, of education for an ever widening market.

5   The resources and facilities of the school should be used for the encouragement of community activity. Continuing education and the social development of the local community is as important as individual education, and association with the local community enlarges the experience of the school.

H5.3: The school curriculum in the years 14–18 will alter to reflect the needs of the changing society. It will be based on:

1   **a common core,**
2   **a wide range of credit-earning optional courses, including**
3   **work experience.**

D5.3:

1   The core, designed to represent a common area of essential experience for this age range, must be seen by students, parents

and employers as relevant to the needs of the individual, the student and society.

The depth and coverage of the core will depend on the ability of the individual student. It will consist of:

- communication skills (listening, speaking, reading and writing);
- skills associated with the retrieval and evaluation of information (qualitative and quantitative);
- skills and concepts associated with investigation, inquiry and judgement;
- number-handling skills and concepts;
- skills and knowledge associated with coping responsibly with the problems of everyday life;
- skills and attributes of personal and physical development.

Between 14 and 18, progressively less time will be spent on the core.

2   Credit-earning optional courses are required because:

- the existing curriculum 14–16 appears to be wide but is actually narrow; although it may contain thirty or more 'subjects', an individual pupil may take only eight or nine;
- courses usually last for two years so it is impossible at present to widen the curriculum, by introducing new subjects, for more than a small minority of students;
- many find two year courses excessively long;
- failure in a two year course frequently carries no credit for what has been achieved.

On the other hand, eight two-year courses may be expressed as sixteen one-year courses, or a greater number of even shorter ones, without any dilution of what in total is offered. Such an arrangement would permit a greater range of curriculum and the opportunity for all students to work at an appropriate level.

We believe that an optional curriculum expressed as 'course units' of approximately thirty hours' duration, or multiples of such units, would achieve greater flexibility and breadth.

Progression from unit to unit, for those able to achieve it, would permit the maintenance, and indeed improvement, of existing standards.

It follows that the schools must establish criteria for course selection, course entrance and course progression in order to provide an integrated and balanced curriculum for each pupil.

This model would be equally appropriate for the 16–18 curriculum which must be capable of meeting the demands of both further education and the world of work and training.

3   Work experience, which we see as a necessary complement to all

full-time education from the age of 14, will form part of the credit-earning optional courses.

Work experience adds materially to the growing maturity and motivation of the young person and creates an involvement in society which could form a valuable bridge between school and work, or school and further education.

H5.4: Achievement within this curriculum will be measured and authenticated by a combination of nationally standardised tests of progress and individual achievement records.

D5.4: GCE and CSE are not capable of assessing and authenticating a student's progress through the curriculum we have outlined for the following reasons:

–   these examinations assess too limited a range of knowledge and learning skills, and certify the standard reached only at the end of a two-year course;

–   for historical reasons, students who have not achieved a grade C in GCE O-level (or grade 1 CSE), are regarded by society as having 'failed'. This implies various degrees of 'failure' for the great majority of students;

–   the present examinations have been constructed in such a way that the grading system works from the highest point of success to the lowest point of failure (i.e. in a negative way), instead of measuring each level of achievment in a positive way;

–   the standard of these examinations is variable: it is related not to absolute criteria of performance, but to a 'pass rate' dependent on the number of candidates entered.

Finally, the present system assumes that all examination syllabuses must contain the equivalent of two years' work at approximately $2\frac{1}{2}$ hours per week. This effectively precludes the modular unit-based curriculum we have outlined.

A student's progress through a given course should be assessed during the course as well as at the end of it. It will be necessary to develop, for each area of the curriculum, an upward progression of nationally standardised tests, in a structure that will permit students to move from one level to another by means of one course-unit of study. Success at each level will be expressed as a pass in a particular 'grade'. The acquisition of such grades should be expressed in terms of credits, and these credits should be recognised when entry levels to subsequent education, training and employment are determined. On this model grades indicate the depth of study, credits indicate breadth.

50

However, such a series of tests of increasing difficulty, for use at different stages in the course, cannot by themselves measure the whole range of qualities and attainments that the curriculum can and should develop. We therefore argue that a record of personal achievment, to which the student may personally contribute, should be maintained by and on behalf of the student during the years 14–16 and 16–18. This record should become the student's property when the student moves from school to the next stage of education, training or work. Employers, professional associations and further education should be consulted about the form this record should take.

H5.5: The methodology of the teaching and learning processes, the pattern of the school day and school year, and the internal and external organisation of the school will all need rethinking if the changing aims and functions of the school are to be achieved.

D5.5

1   In all courses and at all levels we seek a substantial change of emphasis to a learning process that is based upon investigation, analysis and discussion. We look for teaching and learning styles which value doing and understanding, as well as knowing and remembering. The learning process should emphasise the identification of problems, the finding and evaluation of solutions and the taking of appropriate decisions.

The methodology of teaching must:

–   recognise that the size of the learning group should be determined by the nature of the teaching, rather than the subject matter;
–   encourage group learning as well as the development of individual study and learning skills;
–   make appropriate use of available technology.

We argue that, in the teaching and learning process, interaction between student and machine will need to be complemented by a substantial element of interaction between student and student, and between student and teacher.

2   The curriculum we have outlined will require significant changes in the internal organisation of school as follows:

–   new teaching responsibilites will be created and new patterns of staff deployment will be required;
–   the present salary scales and conditions of service will have to be reviewed;
–   new timetabling techniques will be needed;

51

- school rules and rituals will need to be reviewed;
- the school will modify its custodial role, while it develops as a caring and as a learning community.
3 Schools will be accountable through their representative governing bodies (RGBs) to the local community and the LEA. Membership of RGBs will be constituted by representatives of parents, teachers, students, local employers, and members of organisations which make use of the school's facilities, all in a higher proportion to nominees of the LEA.

The RGBs will have power to appoint and dismiss the Head, exercise a general directional control, and provide a consultative forum for management policy. The school should be answerable to the RGB for expenditure of its budget.

4 Nursery schools will be open the major part of the day and for most of the year to be used as needed.

From 5 to 14 the length of the school day and the facilities required will depend on the age of the child. At a stage between 5 and 14, determined by local policy and facilities, a change of school is envisaged. These schools will normally be open all day and during evenings, all the year round, to provide services outlined in 5.2 items 2 to 5.

From the age of 14 there will be increasing emphasis on home- and library-based learning, work experience, and other out-of-school activities, but the school will continue to retain an appropriate share of responsibility for the student's guidance and development, while permitting flexibility in the time of attendance at school. Within this flexibility the community life of the school must be preserved.

5 There is an expectation that there will be enough resources to finance this programme.Buildings are expected to be sufficient in total but considerable updating will be required. Equipment must be also be updated more rapidly to prepare for technology at work.

The current teaching force is sufficient to cover the programme for the reduced number of children per age group. The flexible teaching method outlined envisages differing sizes of teaching group in relation to the teaching style used—lecture, seminar, tutorial, private study. Overall we believe that the pupil-teacher ratio across the whole age range 5–18 should be 15 to 1.

Government finance through the Department of Education and Training will be administered locally by the LEA, including the current activities of the Manpower Services Commission (Training Services Division), which will fund work experience with some help from employers.

We envisage a graduated allowance for young people 14–18, paid initially through parents, and then in progressively increasing proportions to the student/trainee, up to a maximum equivalent to the present £25 per week. The allowance would be conditional on full-time attendance in education/training.

Special points

S5.1: We draw particular attention to our comments on work experience (D5.3 above). We hope that work experience could begin with half a day per week at the age of 14, rising on an optional basis to as high as four days per week at the age of 18.

We are particularly anxious that students on the most academic courses should retain half a day per week or an equivalent block in term or vacation.

The LEA should remain responsible through the school (or college) for the young people concerned; this could include the provision of work experience where necessary.

We would like to see the growth of school-based, profit-earning enterprises (e.g. industrial, commercial, agricultural), and a greater involvement in voluntary work.

S5.2: The provision of appropriate educational computer software is a matter of extreme urgency. Some of the efforts at present being made in this are to be commended, but are now completly inadequate in scale and range. It is now important that schools and teachers clearly define the criteria that software should be meeting.

S5.3: There will be an increasing need for residential school/study centres:
- to serve the needs of those with a temporary or permanent lack of a suitable home base;
- to permit access to a geographical environment or other facilities providing special educational opportunities.

S5.4: It will be important to establish an appropriate range of assessment methods and to avoid undue emphasis on computer marked tests if they do not satisfy assessment criteria adequately.

S5.5: The criteria and mechanisms for national standardisation of grades must be flexible enough to accomodate further initiatives for change in the curriculum content and assessment styles.

General comments

G5.1: The curriculum we have outlined above cannot be implemented without a fundamental change in the present system of examining at 16 and 18 plus.

G5.2: The teaching styles and methods we have outlined, the proposed curriculum framework, and the changed responsibilities of teachers can only be accomplished if urgent attention is given to the way teachers are retrained and trained and to their conditions of service and salary structure.

G5.3: In our discussions we have found that:

–   the usual distinction between 'academic' and 'practical' is irrelevant and damaging to the style of the curriculum outlined;
–   in the age range 14–18, the usual distinction between education and training is unhelpful and unrealistic.

We have assumed that all young people between 14 and 18 will be, in varying degrees, both students and trainees. We believe that the national structure within which education and training are managed should reflect this crucial overlap.

G5.4: We have stressed the importance of universal nursery provision and of a general education to the age of 14 that will be the basis of the years of education and training that follow. This general education should lay the foundation of skills, concepts and knowledge that can enable each individual to reach full potential and make a worthwhile contribution to society.

G5.5: We can find no justification for the present jungle of financial support regulations for young people 14 to 18. All young people of 14 to 18 should be entitled to full-time education/training and, irrespective of parental means, they should receive an education allowance provided they are thus engaged. We have outlined in D5.5 a proposed method of allocation of this allowance.

Recommendations

R5.1: *To the Secretary of State for Education:* The government should immediately abandon the present plans for the merger of GCE and

54

CSE, and announce withdrawal of its support from GCE and CSE as from 1990. It should immediately initiate discussion and implementation of alternative methods of assessment and achievement along the lines described above.

R5.2: *To the Prime Minister:* A Royal Commission should immediately be established to report in 1986 on the supply, training, responsibility and remuneration of teachers.

R5.3: *To the Prime Minister:* A Department of State should be established with a responsibility for education and training.

R5.4: *To the Local Education Authorities:* A priority should be given in allocation of staff and financial resources to the education of the 3 to 14 age group.

R5.5: *To the Prime Minister:* An age-related 'education—and—training allowance', payable for 14 year olds to parents and by the age of 18 to students, should be introduced for all those in full-time education/training. This allowance should replace all allowances and benefits currently relevant to this age group.

CHOICE, COMMITMENT AND CHANGE, 6-18

This paper was written by:
Mr Tim Devlin,
   Director, Independent Schools Information Service
Mr Henry G. Macintosh,
   Secretary, Southern Regional Examinations Board
Mr Hugh J. Sims-Hilditch,
   Managing Director, Marketing and Manufacture,
   Channel Islands
Mr L. C. Taylor,
   Director, Calouste Gulbenkian Foundation, London
Mrs Diana Westlake,
   Waldorf Primary School, Forest Row, East Sussex

under the chairmanship of:
Mr John Sayer,
   Principal, Banbury School, Oxfordshire

Hypotheses and their discussions

H6.1: There will be compulsory education from 6–18.

D6.1: By the year 2000 it is expected that other advanced Western countries will have continued to increase their educational provision for 16–18 year olds. In the developing world twice as many children will be receiving secondary education as at present. British governments will find it politically essential to keep teenage children out of the employment market for as long as possible.

Governments may continue to realise the advantages of providing more nursery education if they are to reduce inequality brought about by different socio-economic circumstances. While some parents will be anxious for their children to start some form of informal or formal

56

schooling as early as possible (for reasons often of convenience), others, probably an increasing few, may wish to use the opportunities provided by the the new technology to provide part of their children's formal education from the resources in the home.

'Education Otherwise' as described in section 36 of the 1944 Education Act could therefore become a much more widely available option. This would make parents more equal partners with the school in the education of their children. This would allow a relaxation in the official starting age for the education process (at present at age five) in favour of a contract between both home and school.

Nursery schools for children aged 3–6 should be available. Parents should be encouraged to use them. The legal requirement on parents to provide formal education for their children (whether at home or at school) should be raised to 6 +.

Towards the end of this century the numbers of school children are expected to rise markedly. Local education authorities may well have to make use of all the educational resources in the community to provide for this increase. They should continue to be responsible for securing the provision of education (and training) by using if necessary a number of other services and agencies including do-it-yourself education schemes, home tutors, and the use of self-financing or partly self-financing education. They would also be using their own programmes via cable television for use in homes, schools, and other centres of education.

Parents should take advantage of the wide ranges of choices open for their children's education. To do this they would need to be properly informed of these choices. Public libraries could be stocked with videotapes illustrating opportunities for education available within the community. Pupils should be encouraged to take increasing responsiblity for deciding their own education after the age of 14. There will need to be some form of control to see that education is provided and made use of. The home/school partnership could be recorded by the school so that it could be checked by local authority advisers. Local authorities should be able to intervene in the interests of the child if the partnership failed to work.

No young person should be allowed to start full-time paid employment until he or she has reached the age of 18. An alternative range of choices should be provided by the authority either from its own resources or by using the resources already within the community. The normal range of choices now available for young people aged 16 and upwards would by the year 2000 need to be available for pupils aged 14 and over. The choices should be extended to include instruction, work experience, day-release, youth training and service to the community outside the school.

57

H6.2: Changes in the nature of home life and employment will require modification to the organisation and character of schools.

D6.2: There will be a large increase in the number of children from one-parent families (1.5 million in 1990 is forecast).

The home will become a less deserted place giving opportunities for a return to more family life with fuller relationships enjoyed between all members of the family. With this in view families should be encouraged financially by home improvement schemes to provide accommodation for permanently retired old or infirm members of the families. This would assist in reducing the dramatic increase in numbers required in social services to look after them. There are existing tax allowances for dependent relatives. Such factors as early retirement, unemployment, job-sharing schemes, short daily working hours and/or a three or four day working week—could have a huge and beneficial effect on bringing the family further together.

By the year 2000 large increases in population are anticipated in the age groups 0–4 (+0.5 million) and 5–10 (+0.9 million). There should be encouragement for adults in the family to teach children at home, as a home-based career, using the technology which will be available to bring a wide variety of learning and interest programmes into the home. The home-based career adults should be helped by tax or other monetary incentives to encourage them.

This would have great advantages: the family structure would be greatly strengthened and present fragmentation of the family life arrested. The home-based adult would ease the unemployment problem; and the educating of children at home would ease considerably the burden on the education system.

The school will be there as required offering both parallel and complementary courses and facilities providing all education for some and some education for all. More particularly the school should have highly specialised facilities, social and artistic activities, vocational training and sports. This would present a slight shift in the roles of school and home and should result in their becoming equal partners. The schools could assist more in providing a sense of corporate identity and community service and will make them still more places of fun, enjoyment and fulfilment.

For the next twenty years there will be an increased interest and participation in the leisure activities for individuals at home (music, TV), at school (sports, art, discussion groups, crafts) and in the community (youth clubs, religious involvement, public and voluntary services). At the

58

request of both parents and children there will be a major growth in special activities such as: camping, weekend and holiday courses and weekly school boarding.

The school with its facilities will become a resource used more on a 24 hours a day, 7 days a week and 52 weeks a year basis by all.

H6.3: New information technologies will change the content and style of education.

D6.3: The 'newer technologies', both 'robotics' and 'informatics', will by AD 2000 have greatly reduced the quantity of paid employment and will have made 'information' available superabundantly—in video and verbal and in passive and interactive forms, in organised courses, remedial sequences, and branching programmes, for encyclopaedic reference, for computer projections, as guidance and control, etc.

At present, one major component in compulsory schooling is the preparation of young people for specific sorts of employment (as distinct from preparation for common experiences in everyday life). Certain skills, certain sorts of knowledge, find a place in the curriculum because they are deemed useful in relation to particular jobs, and they are certificated at a set period as a qualification for a future vocation. There is often an unreal air in such vocationally linked preparation at school. Equipment and subject content gets out of date; skills laboriously acquired turn out to be in declining demand; the attempt to match individuals to a variegated, volatile job-market proves hopelessly speculative. Vocationalism as an incentive requires even now a high degree of make-believe among teachers and taught: it is not likely to survive the added uncertainties and swift transformations the new technologies threaten to bring.

In the short term, the new technologies, by reducing the number of jobs and concentrating power at fewer key positions, seem certain to give a further twist to the competition for success and acquisition, for a declining number of people in a minority of industrially adept countries. In parallel, the first reaction of schools is likely to be a 'hardening' of the curriculum, an increased obsession with getting the available jobs and the better jobs and an enhanced vocational insrumentality. In the long term, however, the newer technologies will presumably dethrone paid employment from the pre-eminence we have given it, simply because its place in the lives of the majority is bound to diminish. At school, preparation for alternatives to full-time employment will become more significant than preparation for specific vocations. The detailed content of the curriculum for individual pupils—the subject of complex combinations, calculations and compromises, referenced to future job utility—may become a matter meriting less anxiety, and education may then centre around fundamental 'arts and habits' acquired and practised through more or less any chosen content. If the period of compulsory common schooling (up to 14) is wholly unconcerned with any future specific vocation, then the provision of a wide range of technical and vocational opportunities beyond 14, and recurrent vocational training throughout a person's working life, will become, by compensation, the more essential.

Those parts of what we learn which can be embodied in symbols and concepts (words, numbers, etc.) will be made accessible, by the newer technologies, outside those large institutions into which, at present, learners must be gathered, since the range of subjects, and grades and sets within them, depends upon how many specialised teachers and matching classfuls of young people can conveniently be assembled in a given place each day. With the information revolution, learning shared between the home, the school and other centres where needed facilities are available, will become technically feasible, and the range of choice, and variations in pace and content within the subjects chosen, will not depend on institutional size. New combinations will become possible of theoretical work done at home or in localised groups, with 'practical' work and periodic classwork done in institutions. 'Informatics' will greatly improve such arrangements, to the point of their becoming a generally available alternative to full-time attendance at schools and similar centres of education.

Beyond the age of compulsory schooling these dispersed arrangements for learning do not require any legal change nor any shift in social attitudes. During the period of compulsion, a baby-sitting role is imposed on the school. In this period, except for young children in 'integrated day' primary schools, the dominant pedagogic method at present (the one around which the school is organised) is class-teaching. The most immediate applications of the newer information technologies are certain to be those which reinforce it. Resources off-air and off-cable, broadcast or pre-recorded, will add a wealth of visual illustration and enrichment to the course the teacher offers, and the television screen of the future will be the means of display for a great variety of 'informatics', and not for broadcasts alone.

Certain specialised applications of 'informatics' will not challenge the central position of class-teaching. For children with handicaps—for the partially sighted, the deaf, for the physically restrained—the newer technologies will be especially helpful. For the slow learner, computer-based learning (CBL), under the control and supervision of a teacher, will offer an invaluable form of one-to-one tutoring providing diagnostic subtlety, patient repetition, adaptability to need, resourcefulness in illustration such as few teachers can rival. CBL will also be useful for short periods of recuperative work (for example, for those who have missed school through sickness) and as a supplement to normal class teaching for any reasonably willing learner who has run into difficulty with some particular patch of learning.

There are, of course, some young people whose self-motivation is such that the uniformities of class-teaching are a frustration, or to whom its character is too public and communal to be attractive. They are especially likely to welcome CBL—for exploring aspects of subjects not covered in the common course, for pursuing subjects too little in demand for their inclusion in the timetable, and for moving at a pace their interest and capacity allows. In terms of school organisation, then, we may expect a school to offer an increased number of subject choices and of optional sections within them.

Yet all the above supports or supplements to class-teaching fall far short of the confident expectations of the prophets of the microprocessor revolution applied to learning. They see an end to the gross inefficiencies of class-teaching entirely. The young will no longer have to be gathered at set times and in set places to hear the ephemeral words of the teacher; they will not have to learn in groups from a source of information—the teacher—able to provide or to arrange only a single course of 'information' which all in the class must try to follow at a common pace. There is no need here to repeat the familiar arguments for styles of learning based on making a provision for individuals, retail, rather than for a class group, wholesale. The newer technology will greatly facilitate these more individualised methods. Sceptics will note, however, that the general availability of varied and permanent sources of information in the form of mass-produced books—a new technology expected in its day to lead to the virtual extinction of verbal teaching—has not greatly changed the dominant style in schools. Computer-based learning will offer ample illustration and animation, provide 'branching' possibilities which the early generation of bone-headed learning machines couldn't physically accommodate, and before long will allow interaction by voice rather than by keyboard. All this may well make computer-based learning more attractive to the young than books; but it too will have to overcome a formidable barrier that has assigned books a minor role and left class teaching unchallenged as the appropriate means of instruction in the secondary school.

That barrier is not lack of appetite or motivation. Most primary schools

61

(in succession to kindergartens) have already adopted a radical alternative to class teaching. An environment has been created in which the child can learn, for the most part, 'informally'—that is, substantially in response to what he or she as an individual finds at that time interesting or stimulating or necessary. It happens, of course, that most of the 'arts and habits' the child needs to learn at this stage coincide with the child's own personal 'curriculum' of informal learning out of school. Moreover, when the child's interest lapses the teacher has, as ally, the relative amenability or gullibility of the young. At the secondary stage things are very different. What has to be learnt reflects other imperatives than individual interest. The experience of daily lessons and of everyday life widely diverge. When self-evident relevance is lacking, sanctions and rewards proliferate. Querulous teenagers asking 'why' are referred to some distant and speculative goal—usually connected with employment, So long as secondary schools are expected to ensure that matters deemed economically, socially, and intellectually 'relevant' by adults shall be learnt within a certain time to a required standard by children, the methods of class-teaching are likely to persist. For being taught in class will remain, for most pupils, the least demanding, most human, dramatic, sociable, and periodically amusing way to fulfil an imposed, extraneous task.

For a primary school child pursuing a chosen thread of learning; for trainees in a chosen job; for students on a chosen course; for adults who choose what they will learn and for all motivated volunteers, the information technologies will provide a highly individualised, devolved and flexible means of learning which will complement powerfully whatever may still be best learnt in groups, and with or from a teacher. In the compulsory period of schooling, so long as the insistence remains on prescribed content to be learnt willy-nilly, and on compulsory schooling as the period of critical allocation (the Grand Shunting-Yard), the newer technologies are not likely to do more than to enrich, and occasionally for special brief purposes to supplement, the staple diet of class-teaching. However, in the longer term, 'robotics' and 'informatics' seem certain to bring about a sharp decline in the place of paid employment in the lifetime expectations of the majority of people. Then, the compulsory school (up to, say, 14), at the secondary as well as at the primary stage, may focus on the development on 'arts and habits'. In that sort of context, the new information technologies elegantly and nicely fit. And if, as we postulate, young people from 14 to 18, although prohibited from full-time paid employment, are offered a wide and varied set of alternatives among

62

which to choose, then the newer technologies will be invaluable as the means of the necessary flexibility, information and control.

H6.4: Post-primary education 11–14 will develop skills of study and decision-making, and the appetite for continued learning.

D6.4: Mathew Arnold suggested that compulsory education was acceptable in Prussia only because everyone there wanted education anyway. Today, parents are required to 'cause their children to receive education', and this receiving becomes all too often a passive mode, the activity being that of the teacher, the class having more or less to follow, especially if all have to reach the same final examination target.

At the primary stage, particularly since the end of the 'eleven-plus', active methods of learning have been developed. They have included skills in the use of a range of resources for information, for selecting and for presenting material. The appetite to learn, so apparent in infant play at home, has been whetted by new resources for discovery and expression. There is much in home, nursery school and primary school learning methods which should be further encouraged and exploited beyond the age of eleven, and which relate to the continuing desire for lifelong learning. Disciplines of learning and modes of thinking are best developed and exercised by memorable experiences rather than memorising, by problem-solving situations which individuals or small teams want to tackle and through which they can be encouraged towards achievement.

In the secondary school remote targets such as a final examination years ahead, used as coercion to accumulate information and to practise its regurgitation in annual school examination sessions, have enslaved schools and scholarship instead of liberating the desire to learn. Moreover, these sequences of aggregated teaching have been channelled through separate subjects masquerading as areas of experience and dominating the formal timetable of secondary schools. Instead of making this worse through an insistence on even greater specialisation in the training of teachers, the school system should signal the breadth of experience and opportunities for enrichment which are there to be enjoyed, 'to have life and to have it more abundantly'. Those aspects of school life which are the most threatened by an impoverishment through insistence on 'basic essentials' and the current siege mentality are the very ones which should form the major contribution of the school to education. Of these enrichment and extension activities, many which are now curiously described as

63

extra-curricular depend upon the voluntary commitment of teachers, pupils and parents, who are able to share and contribute with an ease of relationship made all but impossible in the subject teaching in the classroom. These activities should be seen to be highly valued and no longer regarded as frills.

The school will offer encouragement to develop learning at home and elsewhere, will engage with parents, pupils, and others in the neighbourhood to promote educational opportunities, to discuss worthwhile educational experience from whatever source, and to include these in the school's evaluation of a young person's achievement.

The systematised selfishness embodied in the present public examination system and the spirit derived from success at the expense of others' failure should be countered by praise for activities involving group cooperation and mutual support. These should be overtly esteemed as highly as work done by individuals. The voluntary spirit essential to learning should be fostered by discussion of new targets, leading to a sense of commitment to tasks ahead and loyalty to those who are to share them. Positive and progressive achievement should be recognised at all stages, and not left to a separate final reckoning. Indeed, there should be no appearance of finality in any aspect of study, and no pressure from the school system to discontinue subjects.

The present effects on schools of the higher education system's extreme specialisation must be removed. A school system which enables young people to develop particular talents and aptitudes is one thing; but a pattern which compels them to drop subjects which they want at least to maintain, in favour of narrow specialisation for all, in order that a minority should meet the even narrower requirements of university entrance, is an outrage to any concept of lifelong learning. It may be hoped that the time scales of short intensive higher education, requiring narrowing preparation courses in schools, may be modified as part of a general response to unemployment. Similarly, it may be anticipated that pressure to pursue narrowly vocational courses will be eased, after the initial years of panic, when it becomes clear that direct entry to employment at an early age will be a minority pursuit, and that the skills required for future success in industry are either not specific or are best trained on or from the job.

If schools are to respond to the very different role described, their organisation, staffing and resourcing must be modified according to the intended approaches and outcomes. The use of facilities and time bring with them an expectation of new criteria for staffing. If learning is to be in groups conducive to cooperative and flexible modes of learning, a quite

64

different level and mode of balance of resourcing is to be expected. The classroom has for centuries been determined by the maximum number of children who can be controlled by one adult, and required to receive controlled information at the same time. That will no longer be the prime task of schools or the way they should be organised.

H6.5: Age 14 will be the normal starting point for a wider range of educational alternatives continuing to adulthood.

D6.5: At 14 or thereabouts the child has reached adolescence and is undergoing major physical and emotional development. There is a readiness for change in the style of education, both in regard to the attitude of the teachers and the subject matter offered.

We educate children for the work of the world in its widest sense and the needs are twofold:

1   we should give them the opportunity to unfold the possibilities within their individual natures; and

2   we should prepare them to meet the challenges of social and working life.

These two aims are compatible and complementary.
A healthy balance is of the utmost importance and, in addition to a rich and broadly based programme in the field of sciences and humanities, ALL pupils should engage in a wide range of artistic and practical activities.

The full programme of humanities and sciences together with that of the practical activities would be encouraged for all young people throughout their time at school.

Guided project work of a practical nature and arising from the pupil's interests and capabilities would increase in importance and be taken into account as part of recognised achievement.

Who would be responsible for the 14 to 18 age group?

(a)   The prime legal responsibility below the age of majority would continue to rest with the parent.

(b)   Managerial day-to-day responsibilities for young people up to the age of 14 would be exercised by the school. Over the age of 14, the existing range of institutions and points of managerial responsibility (including the school) which have responsibility at present for children aged 16 and over would have responsibility also for those aged 14 plus. The only exception would be employers, since the 14–18 year olds would not be employable.

(c)   We would want to reinforce a sense of responsibility among

65

parents for their children over the age of 14 and also among the children themselves.

(d)   There would be many adults who could be mobilised for more detailed guidance, counselling, advice and supervision of this age group.

(e)   After 18 this would be a continuous need for everyone at certain times throughout life and that is what community is all about.

H6.6: Local centres of learning and leisure will be needed for all.

D6.6: There is already a large number of institutions providing educational services—schools, youth centres, further and adult education, social service and other allied services of some kind—but they are dissociated from each other. There should be a pooling of resources in a neighbourhood without destroying feelings of separate commitment. This could be done either by schools becoming community centres or by building new learning and leisure centres.

Whatever is decided, provision for the 14 to 18 age group should come under a new form of corporate neighbourhood management to which all available public and voluntary services should contribute.

There should be an overlap between leisure and education. Schools are underused. Their expensive facilities could be made more widely available and those running them could be a combination of qualified and certificated teachers and unqualified enthusiasts. Many schools which become redundant or underused could be converted for this purpose.

By the year 2000 a large number of people will have nothing to do. They should have somewhere to go for education and leisure. They would also provide a potential supervisory force which has so far been untapped.

The proposed corporate management of the community would be separately funded. It should be able to employ both professionals and volunteers. It should identify the needs of the community. There should be a modification of the rating and taxation system to allow members of the public to specify a proportion of the rates for this purpose as they want it.

H6.7: Assessment will need to change in order to match change in the functions and character of education.

D6.7: Any programme of assessment capable of reflecting the kinds of changes likely to take place in education by AD 2000 must:

66

(a)   meet the needs of *all* those involved;

(b)   operate successfully in a wide range of institutions acting on their own or in cooperation;

(c)   promote a continuous programme of self-development through self-evaluation;

(d)   be credible to society as a whole.

Central to meeting these requirements are the following:

(a)   flexibility of operation;

(b)   the creation of structures which take proper account of and hence reflect the full range of individual and institutional interests involved at both regional and national level. At present particular interests—notably higher education—exercise a disproportionate influence;

(c)   the creation of systems for describing and disseminating information about individuals and groups. The nature and range of this information must result from a full discussion between all concerned and ought to reflect at any given time the prevailing view of the character, functions and outcomes of education. The debate must thus be an ongoing one;

(d)   the use of a much wider range of assessment techniques than those currently in general use, with particular emphasis upon informal observation, assessment over time and the continuous measurement of progress;

(e)   a shift in emphasis from reliability to validity and from 'norm' to 'criterion' referencing; that is to say, towards a system which measures individuals against predetermined criteria and not one against another.

In practical terms the realisation of such a programme will demand structures very different from those currently in use: in particular the present public examination model is both inadequate and unable to accomodate the necessary changes. The basic notions which ought to underpin any new system are those of validation and accreditation and the principal role in its development ought to be played by the local education authorities (LEAs), whatever their future form.

Validation is the process whereby approval is given to arrangements for the development of courses of study and their related assessment in accordance with an agreed set of rules or regulations. These rules and regulations may be flexible or prescriptive. Accreditation on the other hand is the process whereby a body grants its imprimatur to other agencies to undertake activities on its behalf. This imprimatur tends to take one of two major forms; a licence to operate, or permission to issue a certificate

67

or some similar award. The granting of both licence and power to certificate can be subject to extremely rigorous conditions including inspection and over the whole process hangs the power to revoke.

Why LEAs? For a number of very good reasons. They currently have statutory responsibility for the control of the curriculum and ought in consequence to be concerned with evaluation; they ought to have the capacity and the wish to mediate between national requirements and local needs; they have the resources, if the will is there to promote staff development without which lasting change is impossible; they have the standing to make locally-based programmes more widely credible; and finally they have the contacts with the local community and local industry whose support is vital if change is to come about.

Recommendations

R6.1: Parents or relatives whose 'career' is to contribute to children's education should receive financial incentives.

R6.2: Nursery education should be available for all children aged 3–6.

R6.3: Primary school methods of learning by discovery should be extended throughout the years of formal schooling from age 6 at the latest through to 14.

R6.4: A new deal is needed to give 14–18 year olds more responsibility for organising their own education along with adults in neighbourhood learning and leisure centres.

R6.5: Training should be extended for all those involved in teaching to take account of the impact of 'robotics' and 'informatics'.

R6.6: No young person should be able to accept full-time paid employment until after the age of 18.

R6.7: The present public examination system should be replaced by one which stresses progressive assessment.

POST-SCHOOL EDUCATION

This paper was written by:
Mr A. George Clarke,
  Principal, Reading Adult College
Mr Frank Fidgeon,
  Technician Education Council
Mr Barry P. Laight OBE,
  Engineering Consultant
Dr David E. Newbold,
  Dean of Education, Huddersfield Polytechnic
Mrs Trish Nicholson,
  Regional Training Officer,
  Highland Regional Council, Inverness
Dr Peter L. Stokes,
  Head of Mathematics and Computer Studies,

under the chairmanship of:
Mr Eric A. G. Morgan,
  Managing Director, British-American Cosmetics Ltd

Hypotheses and their discussions

H7.1: There will be a full-time programme for all 16–18 year olds, involving schools, colleges and industry, and providing a full range of vocational and non-vocational studies.

D7.1: The 16–18 age group is in an area of major uncertainty and indecision in the 1980s. There is now a wide variety of opportunities available to these teenagers. Some of the choices are traditional and well-established, (for example, the multi A-level route to degree courses), whilst others have the appearance of hastily devised expedients, (for example, courses such as YOP (Youth Opportunities Programme), now

69

largely superseded by the more substantial Youth Training Scheme developments). Together all these represent a substantial national investment in 16–18s, but without a coherent structure or a clear purpose. Even within the traditional educational framework, there is widespread confusion among the roles of school sixth forms, colleges of further education, and the new hybrid tertiary colleges. There is insufficient involvement in course design by the customers for the majority of the products of the 16–18 system, that is by industrialists or other comparable employers. They have long expressed concern about the quality of output from schools at 16 +. Without close involvement in a coherent 16–18 plan, they may well be equally dissatisfied with their older, but little better equipped, new employees.

Before AD 2000, a coherent two-year programme for the 16–18 age group will emerge. This will follow directly from a 14–16 programme, which will include options emphasising introductory vocational and industrial studies. The 14–18 programme will appear in many areas as a coherent whole. The 16–18 system will be structured in such a way as to bring together the whole of the age group to meet the needs of those proceeding to higher education, to provide a sound well-prepared and acceptable labour force for industry in its widest sense, to develop a sense of the 'work ethic' in all students, to give students an understanding of the necessity for the creation of national wealth, and to encourage students to take advantage of lifelong opportunities for continuing education. There will be an emphasis on equality of opportunity for men and women, with positive encouragement for both to enter vocations from which they have been traditionally barred, but where they, as individuals, have major contributions to make.

The whole programme will form a complete spectrum, ranging from advanced subject-based courses, at present leading to A-level qualifications (or their equivalent such as Scottish Higher Certificates or the International Baccalaureat), through to vocational courses essentially of a practical nature, which are presently not formally assessed. It will be accepted that all routes through the system which can be chosen by students, will include a vocational element and an academic element, with the balance and standard being moderated according to the aptitudes and abilities of the participants.

Participation in the 16–18 programme will be open to all in the age group, and will be regarded as the normal way in which government finance will be provided. All participants will receive a training allowance, and unemployment benefits will not be available to this age group. It is accepted that it will be necessary to make special provisions for those with

70

mental or physical handicaps, and for those who are temporarily medically unfit, but as far as possible such people will be included in the main programme. A person in this age group who wishes to do so may take up full-time employment, but if he does, he will be required to participate at the employer's expense in a day-release programme.

The standards of the 16–18 programme will be nationally determined. The content will be locally determined and based on a 48-week year, and will include the following elements:

(a)   a flexible subject-based range of choices leading to qualifications for entry to higher education;

(b)   a flexible subject-based range of choices leading to an intermediate standard to support or be complementary to (a) above;

(c)   a flexible vocational range of assessed courses with varying degrees of practical and industrial orientation;

(d)   a range of choices emphasising both literacy and numeracy at a variety of levels;

(e)   a range of choices emphasising community and leisure activities.

Note that ALL students will take at least one choice from among (c), (d), and (e). Not more than 50 per cent of the time will be spent in work experience.

The precise choice of units taken by any particular student will be determined by that student in consultation with an appointed adviser. The two-year programme as a whole will be progressive, so that at the end the student is well equipped either to proceed to subsequent education, or to be employable with particular skills. Educationalists and industrialists will be jointly responsible for the design of the local youth training provision. The location and resourcing of the courses will be determined locally, but will be expected to be based largely on existing school, further education and industrial facilities. The 16–18 programme will operate under a single administrative structure (i.e. not school and further education separately as at present). There will be a substantial interchange of staff between education and industry, both as an aid to the coherence of the structure, and also as a form of development for participating teachers and industrialists.

Whilst it will not be mandatory, all students will be strongly encouraged to undertake a period of residential experience within the 16–18 period as a means of broadening their experience and enriching their geographical and social perspectives.

Students who intend to proceed to higher education will be very strongly encouraged to undertake significant industrial experience beforehand. This may be achieved by a year's work or similar experience as described

71

below (D7.4) or in certain instances by an extended programme in which substantial elements of work experience are located within the normal programme for such students, so expanding it from two to three years.

H7.2: A unified system of higher education will be developed for the over 18s including mature students. There will be strong central encouragement for vocationally related and post-experience courses, especially those which contribute to the creation of national wealth.

D7.2: The overriding aim of the higher education system will be to provide diverse opportunities for learning in a variety of institutions. The ability to benefit will be enhanced by developing a coherent and clear set of connected routes which overcome disparities in regional provision and facilitate access and transfer. Whilst specific traditions are likely to remain and provide continuity, there will be an increasing need for flexibility and innovation to meet the challenges of change and uncertainty. The range of institutions thus envisaged includes universities primarily concerned with pure scholarship, research and teaching.

A binary system (of universities and other higher education institutions) will persist in some form. However, in the face of scarce resources and unused capacity there will be cooperation and collaboration among neighbouring institutions of higher education. The maintenance of academic rigour and excellence is in everyone's interest but a clear need for higher education to adapt to change will continue. A national system will coordinate all existing funding agencies and be thus an efficient way of utilising resources and making accountability more widely applicable.

There will be increased provision throughout the calendar year for mature students to participate in both full-time and part-time courses. The ability to benefit will become the major criterion for admission to all courses, and encouragement to succeed a distinguishing feature.

Clear policies at national level for courses related to wealth creation will be needed. These will take account of both students' and employers' requirements. The challenges of technological developments and ways of utilising scarce resources will provide some motivation to develop the most precious resource, namely the human one. Demands from industry for more appropriately qualified people will increase, and require an expansion of vocational preparation and training courses. The trend towards more efficient and productive use of reduced working hours will be accommodated. Vocationally orientated courses must be characterised both by an excellence of specialisms and breadth of curriculum offerings.

72

In order to enhance their effectiveness vocational courses will have direct relevance to local industries where possible. Courses must be so coordinated through engineering, technical, business and professional councils that standards advance to meet increasing competition.

Curricula will necessarily change to reflect new developments and challenges. The need for flexibility and variety means that short-cycle degree and non-degree courses of two years' duration will become accepted. Broader entry requirements and a modular approach to structured learning as well as open, distance and individualised learning will form part of the pattern of educational and training provision.

In-service courses for teachers and academics will be further developed and will include a management component. The need to adapt and learn from foreign systems will increase. Exchange in industry and education both in the UK and abroad will become a regular occurrence.

Funding for education will be necessarily differential: certain courses may attract larger grants. Loan schemes and bursaries as incentives to train and retrain will be provided.

H7.3: There will be a considerable growth in post-compulsory education and training, especially through part-time courses and activities, not only to improve the quality of life but also to equip people with the skills needed to improve the country's competitive position internationally.

D7.3: To enable society to cope with continuing technological, economic and social change, there will be a comprehensive, coordinated and flexible system of education and training.

At national and local levels many institutions provide between them a wide range of learning opportunities, but often there is no joint planning and little integration.

The numerous barriers to enrolment include lack of information about opportunities, inappropriate entrance requirements, unsuitable timetables, lengthy travel to centres and prohibitive costs. Other factors include fear of 'going back to school', general lack of confidence and the belief that education is only for children. To break down these barriers and to achieve equal opportunities for everyone, we shall have coherent national, regional and local systems of access and counselling.

Considerably more resources will be devoted to increasing the opportunities available, particularly for part-time education and training.

People will need to be trained in the skills required by commerce and industry, to be retrained (possible several times in their lives) for new jobs,

73

and to have training to keep up to date in their work. This continuing training is essential for the development of the skills that will enable us to compete internationally.

There will also be emphasis on general education to achieve levels of numeracy and literacy which will enable more people to progress to further skills.

It will be reasonable and necessary to train people in skills likely to be needed in the medium term and in skills which are gauged to be needed in the longer term. This will include retraining of the unemployed to improve their employment potential.

Many people will have no paid work, and most people will spend fewer hours doing paid work. Everyone, therefore, will need to have the education and training of their choice—for personal development, to increase their self-esteem and to enhance their creative skills. The administrative divisions between vocational and non-vocational activities are being blurred and will disappear.

Special provision for ethnic minorities and for disadvantaged groups, such as the mentally and physically handicapped, and the unemployed, will be greatly increased.

Alternative entry requirements (e.g. based on experience rather than formal qualifications) will be used to make entry as open as possible. As well as traditional courses learning opportunities will include various 'open access' approaches e.g. individualised, independent and distance learning. These offer more freedom and flexibility with regard to learning aims and objectives, methods, pace and location.

Self-help groups of many kinds—study circles, clubs, groups learning practical skills—will be encouraged. Broadcasting and technology will be fully exploited to create new ways of learning.

To provide people with the 'tools' for learning, and to overcome self-doubt, 'how to study' courses, and 'return to study' courses will be provided as essential preparation for education and training.

A comprehensive in-service training system will ensure that educators continually reflect on their work, and are equipped to carry out needed changes.

To deliver this greatly enlarged education service, more accommodation will be required. Multiple use will be made of existing premises, and buildings no longer needed for schools will be used for adults. In each area there will be a network of local education centres for adults. Education and training which is relevant to the needs and aspirations of individuals will motivate them to take part and to benefit themselves and society.

Learning will be promoted as a valuable and enjoyable activity which

74

everyone will care about and undertake in the interests of all. Effective market research will be vital at national and local levels to measure demand. Educational and training agencies will then plan the provision, with representatives from industry and commerce. Joint marketing campaigns, and local information advice and counselling services, will be mounted to ensure that everyone understands what is available and the benefits to be obtained.

H7.4: There will be a minimum annual entitlement to education/training leave for all employees.

D7.4: If social and economic stability is to be maintained during the year 2000 and beyond, then positive action must be taken to increase the resourcefulness, resilience, and adaptability of the population, both as a workforce and in terms of personal and community development. This will require not only a greater proportion of wealth to be invested in human resources, but also that peoples attitudes towards training and education lead them actively to seek and create opportunities for personal enhancement.

Education and training will need to be seen as a continuing process throughout life for all members of society and not just a minority. This principle will be established during working life through greater participation of all sectors of industry and commerce, who will recognise their shared responsibility for the development of human resources in general.

Paid education/training leave of a minimum of three weeks' equivalent per year is envisaged. There will be appropriate arrangements for the accumulation and/or alternative distribution of that time over a number of years. Exemptions will be possible, for example, in situations where an individual already has leave to participate in appropriate community/public service activities, and also in certain occupations where the extent of paid leave is already in recognition of the fact that some of that time will be taken up in further education and training. As it will be a statutory duty upon employers to provide leave and to pay for the activities involved, financial recognition will be given by the government through taxation arrangements.

The content of education/training periods will be agreed between employer and employee. It will not necessarily be job-specific, and will not replace normal on-the-job training given by employers. The establised guidelines will ensure that the best use is made of resources. In most instances the content will be broadly vocational, to up-date and widen knowledge and experience in the same, or related, occupations in the

75

United Kingdom and abroad, through a variety of means including inter-industry and inter-national exchanges. General educational and community pursuits will also be considered of value, in what is intended to be an enriching experience of mutual benefit to the individual and society. Whilst these activities will not necessarily result in the award of any specific qualification, the experience and knowledge acquired will be documented as part of a continuing record of achievement.

In addition, a government-funded scheme will be developed to provide similar opportunities for the unemployed. The increase in provision and access in the field of education for adults, discussed under hypotheses above, will provide a key resource for the activities undertaken during education/training for the employed, the unemployed and the unwaged.

A valuable extension to this scheme would be the addition of a non-compulsory whole year of vocational training or community service. This 'sabbatical' would be applicable to people in all levels of employment to give an opportunity for prolonged or in-depth study or service. It would also be suitable for students who would benefit from a year out of a strictly academic atmosphere before going on to higher education. Such a scheme would require special funding.

H7.5: For every course undertaken a student will receive documentary evidence indicating the nature and level of his attainment.

D7.5: At present, a substantial number of people leave the education system without a certificate or record of achievement. They suffer from a widespread sense of failure and are often unwilling to attempt any further formal education or training. The loss of motivation and potential productivity is enormous. It would be advantageous to move to a system which recorded whatever successes or attainments a student had achieved. This would be more likely to induce a sense of self-esteem and confidence. It would also provide educators and employers with much more information about the skills and attainments of an individual. Employers in particular require relevant information (and a clear understanding of it) about candidates as a basis for recruitment and training.

There will be increasing demand to devise national systems of assessment which are constructive and easy to understand. There will be a need to denote levels of attainment for all subjects studied. Whatever level a student reaches will be recorded to his credit (similar to the present possibility of an O-level being awarded to a student who just fails to achieve an A-level).

This will lead to an increase in the number of courses constructed on a modular basis—although it is recognised that this may not be feasible for some degree courses. On the other hand there may be some vocational and recreational courses which are simple unit modules in themselves. Many vocational courses are susceptible to 'profiling' by recording the detailed elements of attainment.

The modular approach will facilitate the transferability of 'credits' from one course to another. This practice is likely to increase. In other cases transcripts of courses will be made available so that the appropriate level of exemptions in other courses can be assessed.

Certificates of achievement will confer appropriate status on their holders and these will be increasingly recognised on an international basis. There will be national bodies to set and maintain standards. They will work alongside self-validating bodies (such as universities) and will be concerned to ensure that there is minimal confusion of standards. It will be essential to ensure that systems which are increasingly 'open-access' maintain their standards. The certification definitions must be as rigorous and unambiguous as possible.

General comments

G7.1: The human resource remains our most precious asset and any new policy must recognise that both wealth creation and excellence in education derive from this.

G7.2: As success is such a powerful human motivation the design of courses and their assessment should emphasise personal achievement rather than failure.

G7.3: Opportunity and encouragement should be given to all citizens to develop their full potential by participating in post-school education.

Recommendations

R7.1: The present chiefs of major educational, training and industrial bodies should urgently form an executive board, reporting to the Prime Minister, with the remit to arrive, by 1988, at a master plan for the coordination and assessment of all programmes of education and training, for full implementation by 1995.

MECHANISMS OF CHANGE

This paper was written by:
Miss A. E. Adams,
  Editor Inspection and Advice,
  formerly General Inspector, Surrey County Council
Mr Neil Chapman,
  Head Master, Tanbridge House School, Horsham
Mr Handel Davies CB,
  formerly Director of British Aircraft Corporation
Dr Brian W. Kington,
  Industry Liaison Officer, Society of Education Officers
Mr A. John Waddington,
  Manager, Management Resources, Guest Keen and Nettlefolds

under the chairmanship of:
Mr Tim R. P. Brighouse,
  Chief Education Officer,
  Oxfordshire County Council

Hypotheses and their discussions

H8.1: The existing arrangements for the delivery of the education service are a satisfactory framework for change.

D8.1: The distribution of powers and duties under the 1944 Education Act provides a satisfactory framework for present and future developments. Within that legal framework change may be initiated at every level: student, teacher, governor, local authority and Department of Education and Science.

The first thirty years after the 1944 Act were a period of great expansion. Nursery education was established, primary schools were liberated from the 11 + examination, the school leaving age was raised

79

twice, secondary education was made available to all, further and higher education were extended to an ever-widening population, teacher training was lengthened and new universities and polytechnics were established. All this growth and development took place within the framework of the 1944 Act and was possible because the economy was flourishing.

Current criticism of education has arisen in the context of major social and economic changes, both national and worldwide, for which no educational system can be held responsible. In particular the collapse of the youth employment market has taken place in every developed economy and is not peculiar to Britain. In this connection there should be a wider recognition of the limits to change which education alone can make in any society. Many other powerful institutions including the mass media, trade unions and multi-national companies, may have greater impact on society, while at times being at variance with the work of teachers.

Accordingly the money needed to correct the faults in the present system of education should be under the control of those exercising legal powers and duties in education.

Whether or not the public examination boards are to be regarded as an integral part of the present arrangements there is no doubt that they exert an inordinate influence upon the organisation and curriculum of secondary schools and place a serious financial burden on local education authorities. The same investment of time and money as now mainly benefits these examination boards could be used for other purposes, for example to sustain the validation of individualised courses of study and the accreditation of more of the outcomes of compulsory education. Recent initiatives taken by the Oxford Delegacy of Examinations suggest that even these institutions can act as catalysts of change.

There is a contrary view. The education system is an intricate system of checks and balances which has survived wave after wave of criticism, from whatever quarter it has come. Major institutions tend to suffer from inertia and cultural lag unless constant re-examination and renewal are built into their structures. Further the teaching profession is resistant to change mainly because teachers are locked into a structure controlled by public examinations.

The present arrangements have been the framework within which several major changes in education have actually occurred since 1944. It is far from proven that the system's apparent lack of response to change in recent years is the result of its own insufficiency or inertia rather than caused by the country's economic decline and the consequent reduction of investment in education.

H8.2: The problems of the educational system in providing an appropriate response to change will be increasingly aggravated by the accelerating pace of change, and require either a responsiveness implied but often unrealised in the present arrangements, or a change in those arrangements themselves.

D8.2: The existing arrangements, designed for a period of planned growth without the expectation of serious instability, were an adequate framework for a number of major changes and developments in education. However, there were serious gaps in educational response to changes which were, in some quarters, the subject of valid criticisms even before current economic and social pressures brought them forcibly to the surface. We refer, for instance, to the introspection of the teaching profession, which inhibited the recognition, as it was occurring, of change relevant to education. We refer also to the way in which the content of examination syllabi and the methods of assessment cause a concentration on the pursuit of factual knowledge. At the secondary level, this led to the suppression of the development of those skills, creativity and competence which are primary requirements in post-school life. The need from now on will be for a framework capable of producing an appropriate and rapid response in circumstances that make planned growth/development on a large scale or over a long period inappropriate if not impossible. The system must include mechanisms for constant re-examination and renewal. Even the foreseeable changes in technology, the economy and society will produce a formidable task not only for education but for other major social institutions. The unforeseeable changes on the other hand may require of us all even greater adaptability.

Faced with such a situation, the educational system may have to adandon the traditional and choose a more participatory model. In the traditional model, a national framework of changes is drawn up by a team of senior managers or 'experts' and an attempt is then made through consultation and exhortation to have the plan accepted and implemented at lower levels. It would be highly risky, to say the least, not to learn from the previous failures in education elsewhere to innovate using this model. The major lesson to be learned from both the curriculum projects of the 1960s and 1970s in England *and* from the earliest Scottish attempts in a centralised system to introduce examination and curricular reforms is that change must be initiated by the key agents of change, namely, students and teachers in classrooms.

This brings us to a discussion of the participatory model, by which we mean that change is best effected by involving from the very beginning the ideas, commitment, and expertise of all those involved at all levels. Both the Scottish system and the Schools Council in England have moved—through dint of hard experience—to working within this model.

Education is everybody's business and the more informed and involved people are—not only students and teachers, but parents, employers, and administrators—the more appropriate are the remedies likely to be. Above all, in classrooms, lecture halls, laboratories and training centres, young people have to be committed to their studies and work: and to feel that they have negotiated the educational course best suited to their needs.

The new role for teachers would be as facilitators of learning, negotiating individualised curricula with their pupils. This process will involve pupils in a wide range of problem solving skills of the kind that this society will need to cope with new tasks. What education has to attempt is to enable young people to grow up with confidence in their own qualities and abilities and with something to show as evidence of their competencies.

In other words, if change is to be lasting and effective, teachers must be involved in its prescription and in its implementation. If they are to stimulate that change both at the right time and in the right direction they must be equipped with sufficient knowledge and understanding of the society which requires it. It is not sufficient that their dissatisfaction with present arrangements should relate only to the education system itself nor even to society as it is perceived from the classroom. It must derive from an informed view based on experience, of society and education's place within it.

General comments

G8.1: We are convinced that there are many ways to effect change and yet preserve stability of personal relationships amongst those involved.

G8.2: Change—other than of a cosmetic nature—will not be effected unless four features are present at the same time:
- dissatisfaction with present arrangements;
- a shared view of a desired future state;
- a knowledge of a few first steps;
- participation at all levels in the process of change.

G8.3: Falling rolls and economic constraint provide catalysts for change in a way that the expansion of the service did not.

82

G8.4: Change is influenced not only by resources—including the lack of them—but also the mechanisms by which they are distributed. A system of bidding against agreed priorities can be more effective than a system of predetermined allocations.

G8.5: The timing and combinations of the various recommendations for change are important and require the most skilled and sensitive leadership on the part of those involved.

G8.6: The agencies which have already done a great deal to influence attitudes and to stimulate change should be held forward as models of good practice and their achievements widely communicated.

G8.7: Institutions, individuals, or LEAs operating in isolation are unlikely to be as effective as they would be if they were interdependent. Moreover, since existing vested interest groups are powerful inhibitors of change the creation of new networks to support change is important.

G8.8: We would like to emphasise that many of our recommendations, although listed separately, are interdependent. For example, changes in curriculum and assessment necessitate a large-scale programme of in-service training for teachers.

Recommendations

R8.1: That the accreditation of the outcomes of compulsory education, including the existing examination system at $16+$, be the subject of fundamental change so that all youngsters' talents—practical, social, physical, emotional, aesthetic as well as academic—be assessed by appropriate and different methods. The curriculum, relevant in content and method, must involve the individual young person as an independent learner preparing to cope in a rapidly changing world. The new assessment system will need to be comprehensive, comprehensible and worthy of the respect of parents, students, teachers, industrialists, and the staff of further and higher education. (Action: DES, LEAs, Secondary Examinations Council.)

R8.2: That the initial and in-service education of teachers be reformed to accord with the new demands made of teachers by the first recommendation and in particular that attention be given to collective and institution-based in-service training. (Action: LEAs, HMIs, schools, providing agencies including employers.)

R8.3: That attention be given to the deployment of staff, the grouping of pupils, the planning of the timetable, the flexible use of time and accomodation if desired change is to be reinforced. (Action: LEAs, schools, colleges, universities, polytechnics and DES.)

R8.4: That the role of parents as complementary educators be better recognised. (Action: LEAs, schools, teacher associations.)

R8.5: That governing bodies, reconstituted where necessary to represent a broader cross-section of the community, be encouraged to exercise the powers already vested in them. (Action: DES, LEAs, schools.)

R8.6: That more resources be made available to primary education to ensure maximum achievement in literacy and numeracy. (Action: LEAs.)

R8.7: That institutions be given more power of decision over their own resources. (Action: LEAs.)

R8.8: That steps are taken to emphasise in the education of all the mutual responsibilities of schools, colleges, and the various elements in their associated communities (e.g. commerce, manufacturing industry, government agencies and trade unions). (Action: employers' organisations, LEAs, schools, FHE.)

R8.9: That all the central funds available for education and training (funds which at present come from a variety of government departments) should be controlled by a new unified Department of State for Education, Science and Training. (Action: government.)

R8.10: That there be an evaluation system established for all educational institutions and individuals within them. (Action: LEAs, teacher associations, schools.)

R8.11: That a system of continuous evaluation be built into the changes proposed above; and that existing research funds for education be largely diverted to this purpose. (Action: DES, SSRC, LEAs, universities, NFER.)

84

THE CHALLENGE OF CHANGE

This paper was written by:
Mr Mervyn Benford,
   Head teacher Lewknor Primary School
Mrs Susan Fey,
   Principal, Tunbridge Wells Adult Education Centre
Mr Peter Flowerday,
   Assistant Director, Middlesex Polytechnic
Dr John Gilbert,
   Senior Lecturer in Science Education, Institute of Educational Development, University of Surrey
Mr Quentin M. Thwaites,
   Head of Dept of Mathematics,
   St George's R.C. School, London

under the chairmanship of:
Dr Ray M. W. Rickett,
   Director, Middlesex Polytechnic

Hypotheses and their discussions

H9.1: The individual has always has been the focus of education. The prime challenge for the future will be the greater recognition of this fundamental concept through changed priorities and practice.

D9.1: While affirming the position of the individual, it is recognised that individual development is enriched by the knowledge and experience of others.

H9.2: To meet the needs of personal development in a rapidly changing technological society, greater emphasis will be placed on the acquisition of concepts and essential skills, including those of learning and of living in the community.

D9.2: Education is an experience by which we all seek the levels of personal competence and security necessary to lead useful and satisfying lives. In an ever-expanding world of knowledge the imperative must be to equip people with the skills to produce, acquire and use knowledge as they need it.

There must be recognition of the impact that personal circumstances have on learning.

A particularly damaging feature of present practice is the excessive fragmentation of learning into subjects. Teachers should treat knowledge in an integrated fashion to reflect life.

There is a culture to do with making, managing and organising that elevates particular skills of decision-making and responsibility. This can only enhance an individual's competence and should find expression in what is required in education.

Increasing, and conflicting, external demands upon curricula, time and priority cannot realistically be met. This argues powerfully for a general curriculum, broad and liberal in essence. It should be less committed to the storing of knowledge than at present, and more concerned with activity, problem-solving, intellectual and social skills.

H9.5: Educational institutions will become centres of learning motivator.

D9.5: The traditional notion of teaching, for whatever purpose, the rest of this century and beyond, will be to change the quality and character of what happens daily in our schools.

For those students who can realistically expect to obtain access to higher education, current schooling can have some identifiable extrinsic motivation. However, for the great majority of students the curriculum must have an intrinsic motivation, i.e. its content and methods must have a real personal and practical value. This can be especially true for those who may not subsequently have paid employment. The intrinsic worth of the curriculum should be recognised by all students and staff alike.

86

H9.4: By AD 2000, education will be perceived by most members of society as a lifelong process; society will expect increased access to education outside the ages of compulsory schooling.

D9.4: It is probable that there will be increasing awareness of the value of education, not merely as offering enhanced chances of employment, but as a means of self-fulfilment. A smaller proportion of time will be devoted to traditional 'paid employment' although most people will be involved in 'work' whether traditionally paid or organised around other incentives. It will become increasingly unusual to have one type of job for life. In addition, many people are likely to experience periods of their working lives without paid employment. 'Early' retirement will become the rule rather than the exception. There will be greater awareness of the importance of pre-school education and increased pressure for adequate provision.

The so-called 'less able' members of our society are likely to be most affected by the changing nature of employment. The jobs they have hitherto been able to obtain may no longer exist. Increased access to education can provide not only a means to acquire essential personal skills, but also community activities designed to improve the quality of life and relieve feelings of isolation.

Increased access does not simply refer to an increased availability of educational premises. It implies the removal of other barriers to educational and training opportunities, viz. finance, location, knowledge of opportunities and modes of learning. There will, in addition, need to be involvement of the participants in the planning and execution of the educational process.

H9.5: Educational institutions will become centres of learning and social activity within the community.

D9.5: The traditional notion of teaching, for whatever purpose, depends on the idea of 'the class'. Overwhelming evidence has accumulated which refutes the expectations on which the idea of the class rests, i.e. it has been found that students invariably have diverse prior knowledge and skill of the subject; they have a wide variety of aims in view when learning; their expectations of attainment are varied; and they learn in significantly different ways.

If the notion of 'the class', with its implication of lock-step progress, is abandoned, the possibilities of seeing learning as central force of the

87

educational endeavour and the individual as the instigator and client, can be realised. Thus systems are needed which allow individuals to pursue identified goals, by methods they find valuable, at convenient times. Attainment should be measured, in the first instance, against their own standards. Educational provision will be made for the needs of the individual, rather than the individual meeting the needs of the system, which is often the case now.

The ritualistic elements of educational establishments will be subordinated to the processes of learning. Using a wide variety of techniques for the facilitation of learning, including the employment of teachers, these centres of activity will be open at times which reflect the social circumstances of clients. The identification and pursuit of learning goals, negotiated between the clients and the institutions, will be their principal purpose for existence.

Existing educational establishments should become learning centres, and their employees retained as 'facilitators'. This will require a new approach to the use of premises and resources, through expanded demand to more efficent use.

H9.6: In the year 2000 there will still be ethnic minority groups living in communities isolated from the rest of the population. The problems this presents to the educational system will not have been resolved.

D9.6: It is possible that ethnic minorities will continue to be more drastically affected by unemployment than others and will suffer poverty and deprivation to a greater degree. Already some of the younger members are rejecting the values of our society in general, and education in particular, as being irrelevant to them and ineffective in fulfilling their needs. It is true to say that they hold these views in common with some younger members of the rest of the population but it is emphasised by nature of their ethnic minority status.

We need to develop trust and confidence in a system which currently is not succeeding in either of these areas. Particular care should be taken to detect and remedy under-achievement.

Failure to attend to the needs of any disaffected group in society in general, and ethnic minorities in particular, can but adversely affect society as a whole and impose a great strain upon the traditional notion of tolerance in this country.

to appropriate areas of progress. Thus it is likely that self-assessment will normally be used in conjunction with external assessment.

It is considered that most examinations do not adequately measure achievement in a clearly defined context. Furthermore, there can be no doubt that the curriculum and modes of learning in many schools are severely inhibited by the extensive system of public examinations.

However, there are examinations which do efficiently serve a well-defined and needed purpose. These include 'graded tests' which normally:

(a)   demand a high rate of positive achievement;

(b)   test a narrow range of abilities;

(c)   may be taken at any time of life and indeed quite frequently in any one year.

Graded tests could be introduced in more subject areas during the compulsory ages of schooling. Such tests should be used to motivate the student, and might even provide a continuation point for further education later in life. In certain subject areas these tests could be used by students to demonstrate a level of achievement to employers.

Abilities such as problem-solving, group work, leadership, initiative, data skills, lateral thinking and other intellectual skills will be increasingly valued and nurtured in education. It is in qualities such as these that many employers seem to assess applicants by looking at their job applications and/or by interviewing. These abilities are perhaps the intellectual expression of the personal characteristics that an employer seeks. It is essential to have a system for assessing such skills.

As regular participation in further education increases it is likely that many short courses will result in some form of certificate of achievement as evidence of meritable participation.

In conclusion, traditional forms of examination, as the main method of assessment, are inefficient and unlikely to remain, and will be replaced by a combination of graded tests, self-assessment techniques, profiles and certificates.

H9.12: The place and purposes of examining boards will be more closely attuned to overall educational needs.

D9.12: The present GCE A-level examining boards are predominantly geared to the entry requirements of higher education and O-level examinations reflect the same concerns and patterns. Currently only some 12 per cent of each age group entering secondary education proceed to higher education. Nevertheless, the curriculum for all those in schools is strongly influenced by that small minority. If schools examining boards did not also seek to serve the function of higher education selection, there would be great benefit for all.

H9.13: Educational establishments will become subject to closer scrutiny and assessment.

D9.13: There should be careful study of the forms that such assessment might take; it is likely that insitiutional self-assessment will increasingly be required.

H9.14: The successful implementation of change will require:
(a) **a commitment to search for the views of the individual;**
(b) **political will;**
(c) **industrial support;**
(d) **professional consent.**

D9.14: The changes required are so far-reaching and all-embracing that we will need fully to explore the existing methods of consultation and beyond these, to develop broader-based methods which could involve the whole population.

If the necessary changes are to occur, local and national politicians of all parties will need to be convinced that these developments are congruent with the best interests of constituents and party philosophies.

Industry and commerce, including trades unions, will have to be assured that as the educational system evolves it will supply the necessary flow of skilled manpower to achieve industrial objectives.

This will be built on the widespread recognition by teachers and central/local government administrators that the present system is inadequate. Their personal commitment to change will restore the professional dynamic to education.

Recommendations

R9.1: All educators must be prepared for a changing role in which they guide and facilitate as well as teach. Students should have more opportunity to manage their own learning which should emphasise activity and experience across subject boundaries.

R9.2: School, home and industry must work more closely in the conduct of the students' learning. Teachers must recognise the many ways that students' experience can be enriched and professionalism enhanced by parents, industrialists and others.

R9.3: All entrants to teacher education courses must have had at least two years of employment outside education, whilst at all levels of education teachers must have not less than six months' employment outside education in every seven years' service.

R9.4: There must be more positive effort to encourage members of ethnic minority groups to participate at all levels throughout the education system.

R9.5: Increased access to educational establishments demanded by a lifelong education system must be supported by appropriate changes in the organisation, management and funding of these establishments. Such arrangements must include the provision of education and training advisory services for the whole community.

R9.6: The legal requirements for the provision of education and training should be extended to include the needs of the pre-school child and the adult population whether in paid employment or not.

R9.7: Employers must be given a role in providing for the continuing education of their employees with financial incentives to support this commitment.

R9.8: A system of individual assessments must be developed that enhances the awareness, satisfaction, motivation and progress of the individual and that enables the individual to demonstrate a level of achievement in any field to a third party.

R9.9: A schools examining board should be concerned exclusively with the general educational needs of school-leavers. A higher education entry board should be established to deal with the needs of those who, having completed the final stage of schools examinations, wish to prepare for entry into higher education.

R9.10: All levels of education should be funded by earmarked grants which would include a guaranteed threshold of educational provision within a rational framework.

R9.11: The consultation about Education 2000 should be organised and developed in such a way that it will involve not only recognised and established groups, but any individual who wishes to put forward a point of view.